Young Meaning Makers

Teaching Comprehension, Grades K-2

D. RAY REUTZEL
SARAH K. CLARK
CINDY D. JONES
SANDRA L. GILLAM

Foreword by P. David Pearson

TEACHERS COLLEGE PRESS

TEACHERS COLLEGE | COLUMBIA UNIVERSITY
NEW YORK AND LONDON

Published by Teachers College Press, 1234 Amsterdam Avenue, New York, NY 10027

Copyright © 2016 by Teachers College, Columbia University

Cover design by Rebecca Lown Design. Photo by Robert Kneschke, Shutterstock.

Grateful acknowledgment is made for permission to reprint the following:

Excerpt from Clyne, M., & Griffiths, R. (2005). *Sand*. Parsippany, NJ: Celebration Press–Pearson Education Group. Used by permission of Pearson Education, Inc. All Rights Reserved.

Figure 1.8 from Fisher, D., & Frey, N. (2015). Contingency teaching during close reading. *The Reading Teacher* 66(4), 277–286. Copyright © 2015. Reproduced with permission of John Wiley & Sons, Inc.

Excerpts from *From Tadpole to Frog* by Jan Kottke, © 2000 by Rosen Book Works, Inc., and reprinted with permission.

Excerpts from *From Cocoa Bean to Chocolate* by Robin Nelson. Text copyright © 2003 by Lerner Publishing Group, Inc. Reprinted with the permission of Lerner Publications Company, a division of Lerner Publishing Group, Inc. All rights reserved. No part of this text excerpt may be used or reproduced in any manner whatsoever without the prior written permission of Lerner Publishing Group, Inc.

Library of Congress Cataloging-in-Publication Data

Names: Reutzel, D. Ray (Douglas Ray), 1953–, author
Title: Young meaning makers : teaching comprehension, grades K–2 / D. Ray
   Reutzel, Sarah K. Clark, Cindy D. Jones, Sandra L. Gillam.
Description: New York, NY : Teachers College Press, 2016. | Series: Common
   core state standards in literacy series | Includes bibliographical
   references and index.
Identifiers: LCCN 2016004245 (print) | LCCN 2016016278 (ebook) | ISBN
   9780807757604 (pbk.) | ISBN 9780807757611 (case) | ISBN 9780807774731
   (ebook)
Subjects: LCSH: Language arts (Elementary)—United States. | Language arts
   (Elementary)—Standards—United States. | Common Core State Standards
   (Education)
Classification: LCC LB1576 .R48 2016 (print) | LCC LB1576 (ebook) | DDC
   372.6/2—dc23
LC record available at https://lccn.loc.gov/2016004245

ISBN 978-0-8077-5760-4 (paper)
ISBN 978-0-8077-5761-1 (hardcover)
ISBN 978-0-8077-7473-1 (ebook)

Printed on acid-free paper
Manufactured in the United States of America

23 22 21 20 19 18 17 16   7 6 5 4 3 2 1

Contents

Foreword

A time-worn phrase in our society is: "Everyone TALKS about the weather but nobody seems to DO much about it." The same could be said about Standards in the field of education: "Everyone TALKS about the standards but nobody seems to DO much about them."

The difference, of course, is that while we really can't do much about the weather, we really can do a lot about the standards, especially the Common Core State Standards (and all of their kissing cousins in those states that opted out of the CCSS). We can design curriculum, pedagogy, and activities

- to bring them to life in classrooms and schools,
- to make them tools of progress rather than barriers to progress for teachers and for students and their families, and
- to seriously prepare students for college and career—and citizenship.

And what better time and place to start doing something about these standards than with 5- through-8-year-olds inside our primary grade classrooms? That's exactly the outrageously and delightfully ambitious goal that Ray Reutzel, Sarah Clark, Cindy Jones, and Sandra Gillam have set for themselves and, by implication, for us as their colleagues in *Young Meaning Makers*, which is all about how to teach and foster the development of text comprehension in grades K–2.

If their goal is to help K–2 teachers get young students off to a flying start on becoming close, careful, and critical readers of fiction and nonfiction, their approach is to ground everything we do in our schools—the materials we have kids read, the instructional guidance we provide, the activities we ask them to do, and the tools we use to assess their understanding—in what is arguably the most complete and empirically validated theory of reading comprehension we have had to date in the fields of cognition and education. They are clearly betting on Kurt Lewin's famous adage, "Nothing is as practical as a good theory" (Lewin, 1952).

And they manage to pull it off! *Young Meaning Makers* is as practical as it is theoretical. And because it is both, teachers not only get a lot of very practical teaching ideas, they get it always packaged in a framework that surrounds, gives credence to, and explains why any given lesson, activity, or assessment is being used with these types of students at exactly this point in their development. Thus teachers are not subservient to the particular set of exemplar lessons that they get in the book (and, by the way, those lessons are great in their vivid detail and rationale); the theory that those lessons exemplify are levers for developing new and different lessons for new and different texts and students.

The authorsy do a great job of elaborating on Kintsch's theory of comprehension (1988), which Kintsch dubbed the Construction-Integration (C-I) Model, in ways that resonates for both novice and expert teachers. They then link the stages of the C-I Model as follows:

1. Construct a textbase by building both a microstructure and a macrostructure for the text
2. Integrate prior knowledge and the current textbase to create a situation model
3. Integrate that newly minted knowledge in the situation model into existing knowledge stored in memory

Then the cycle starts all over again, but at this point with a knowledge base that is even richer than before because it includes that knowledge the reader just acquired through reading and understanding. Borrowing from my colleagues and I (Duke, Pearson, Strachan, & Billman, 2011) Reutzel and his partners refer to this as a virtuous cycle in which knowledge begets comprehension begets learning begets knowledge, anon, anon, anon.

This book is all about making that model come to life with lively activities taught by lively teachers to lively readers. So read this it with the gusto it provides and deserves, and go out into your classrooms and make texts come to life through the magic of understanding!

Finally, enjoy your journey through this book! I did!

P. David Pearson
Evelyn Lois Corey Professor of Instructional Science
Graduate School of Education
University of California, Berkeley

REFERENCES

Duke, N. K., Pearson, P. D., Strachan, S. L., & Billman, A. K. (2011). Essential elements of fostering and teaching reading comprehension. In A. E. Farstrup & S. J. Samuels (Eds.), *What research has to say about reading instruction* (4th ed.). Newark, DE: International Reading Association.

Kintsch, W. (1988). The use of knowledge in discourse processing: A construction-integration model. *Psychological Review, 95,* 163–182.

Lewin, K. (1952). *Field theory in social science: Selected theoretical papers by Kurt Lewin.* London, England: Tavistock.

Preface

With this book, we hope to clarify how the Common Core State Reading Standards (CCSS) for teaching literature and informational texts were meant to be understood and implemented by classroom teachers during comprehension instruction. If one reads the documents describing the CCSS for reading, reading comprehension instruction seldom if ever is mentioned. The curious absence of the ultimate objective in reading instruction—comprehension—in the standards' documents at first raised concerns among practitioners and scholars alike. How could comprehension instruction not have a clear and obvious presence in the CCSS Reading Standards?

There are at least two plausible explanations for the seeming inattention to the centrality of comprehension instruction in the CCSS. First, the CCSS assiduously avoided replicating the structure of the five elements of reading instruction so prominently practiced as insular components as a result of the Report of the National Reading Panel (2000). These CCSS Reading Standards were designed expressly to integrate the five components of effective reading instruction the NRP reported out. They were not intended to reify the structure and elements of effective reading instruction—phonemic awareness, phonics, fluency, vocabulary, and comprehension—as instructional silos to be taught each day with a designated time allotment and accompanying standards. Second, the CCSS Reading Standards, if properly viewed by professional developers, teachers, and scholars, were intended to send a new message about reading instruction. The Reading Standards were intended to be the *comprehension* standards for learning from literature and informational texts. Furthermore, these *comprehension* standards weren't just a listing of random skills and strategies in comprehension. The standards reading literature and informational text were grounded in a strong theoretical framework that had been empirically studied for many decades. The theoretical framework supporting the CCSS for reading literature and informational text is known as the Construction–Integration Model of Text Comprehension by Dr. Walter Kintsch (2013).

Kintsch's model of text comprehension processes and its connection to the CCSS Reading Standards have been highlighted by Pearson and Hiebert (2015) in *Research-Based Practice for Teaching Common Core Literacy*. Additionally, P. D. Pearson recently highlighted the centrality of Construction–Integration Theory of Text Comprehension processes in his Jeanne S. Chall address at Harvard University (www.gse.harvard.edu/news/15/10/watch-11th-annual-jeanne-s-chall-lecture).

The intent of this book is to show how the content and structure of the CCSS for reading literature and informational text are structured in a tiered sequence of Anchor Standard clusters that mirror the text comprehension processes Kintsch describes in his theory: first, construction of meaning; and second, integration of constructed meaning into the long-term world knowledge and experiential store in the human mind. Beginning with the construction process, the CCSS Reading Standards encompass a cluster of three standards intended to ensure that students are able to determine the key ideas and details represented in text; these three standards correspond with Kintsch's construction of the micro text structure. For students to progress, they must be able to appropriately attend to the elements and ideas presented in the text. Next, the CCSS Reading Standards describe another cluster of three Anchor Reading Standards intended to ensure that students can determine and use the author's craft and structure as represented in text; these standards correspond with Kintsch's construction of the macro text structure. It is here that students determine how the author has crafted the text to include the use of literary devices and text structures to construct an organizational framework (macrostructure) for the key ideas and details (microstructure) in the text resulting in the creation of what Kintsch (2013) calls a textbase or representation of what was in the text. Finally, the CCSS reading standards list a third cluster of three standards intended to ensure that students integrate the ideas represented in the textbase by engaging in Kintsch's integration of the situation model of the text into their background knowledge.

In Chapter 1, we lay out the case for viewing the CCSS Reading Standards through the lens of Kintsch's Construction–Integration (CI) Model of Text Comprehension. We describe how children can be taught to process texts using this theory and how teachers can select and implement the CCSS Reading Standards to match the processes of text comprehension described by W. Kintsch (2013). We do this by comparing the most well-known and -used model of comprehension, schema theory, with CI theory, demonstrating how the CCSS for reading were designed to support, in content and sequence, the CI text-processing model rather than schema theory. We also provide a sample lesson demonstrating how teachers can utilize the CCSS Reading Standards to ensure that students are able to process text at the levels of, first, construction, then, integration.

In Chapter 2, we describe how the CCSS for speaking and listening can be addressed using the CI Model to build an oral language base for use in later text comprehension processes. Research demonstrates a clear and enduring connection between early oral language processing and later reading comprehension ability. This chapter shows teachers of young children how they can begin building text comprehension processes to increase students' oral language comprehension using many of the evidence-based practices that speech-language pathologists use. Sample strategies and lessons are provided using literature and informational text examples.

In Chapter 3, we focus attention on applying the CI Model to the CCSS reading standards for literature. Literature has long played a pivotal role in developing young children's early comprehension. Text selection for developing young children's comprehension using literature, as found in CCSS Reading Anchor Standard 10, is given initial attention in this chapter. Next, we provide sample comprehension lessons for teaching reading lessons using the CI Model and the CCSS reading standards with literature. We begin with constructing microstructure with literature and then progress to constructing macrostructure with literature to create a textbase. After describing the "C" or construction phase of the CI Model, we describe a series of sample lessons for building a situation model that is to be integrated into background knowledge. We wrap up this chapter by discussing the benefits of using a CI Model in conjunction with the CCSS reading standards for literature to develop young students' comprehension of appropriately challenging literary texts. In Chapter 4, we repeat this process with respect to applying the CI Model to the CCSS for reading informational text.

In the final chapter of this book, we turn our attention to assessing young students' comprehension growth through developing formative assessments that probe students' abilities to meet the demands of the CCSS reading standards with literature and informational text at various grade levels and at various stages of the CI Model of Text Comprehension processes. We discuss three ways in which reading comprehension has been assessed in the past: (1) free recall, (2) probed recall, and (3) sentence verification tasks. We discuss the fact that these assessments tend to treat comprehension as a unitary construct. The problem with this approach is that comprehension is anything but a unitary construct. Next, we treat the topic of formative versus summative assessments. Until major assessment producers provide access to formative, benchmarking assessments, teachers will need to know how to make their own. To help teachers, we show how a formative assessment plan based on the CCSS Reading Standards and the CI Text Comprehension Model can be designed. Finally we describe how to develop formative assessment tasks for each of the four stages of the CI Text Comprehension Model: (1) microstructure, (2) macrostructure, (3) situation model, and (4) integration of the situation model into background knowledge stored in long-term memory.

As authors, it is our hope not only that this book will support teachers in providing more theoretically sound, coherent, and effective comprehension instruction, but that our readers will begin to view the CCSS reading standards for Literature and Informational Text as theoretically based and arranged into clusters to be used in an intentional, sequenced, and cogent way, rather than randomly selecting one or more CCSS Reading Anchor Standards and focusing on these throughout the instruction of a text.

If we can help teachers both understand the theoretical structure of the CCSS for reading literature and informational text and that they need to select a standard from each of the three Anchor Standard clusters in order to deepen students' comprehension during subsequent "close readings" of text, we will have succeeded in our objectives for writing this book. Please let us know as you read and use this book your experiences in teaching literature and informational text using the theoretical lens of Kintsch's CI Model of Text Comprehension to select and teach comprehension lessons that meet the integrated, multi-leveled processes encompassed in the arrangement of the CCSS reading standard clusters and anchor standards. Teachers with whom we have worked and who have converted their teaching to the ideas presented in this book tell us that it has changed how they view text comprehension. But most importantly, they tell us it has given them an explanation as to why and how to engage their students in close readings of text to deepen their students' text comprehension.

—*D. Ray Reutzel, Sarah K. Clark, Cindy D. Jones, Sandi L. Gillam*

CHAPTER 1

Comprehension Instruction
The Importance of Theory

There is nothing so practical as a good theory.

—Kurt Lewin

CHAPTER OVERVIEW

Reading comprehension is indisputably the ultimate objective of reading instruction and constitutes the very essence of the act of reading (Duke, Pearson, Strachan, & Billman, 2011; Durkin, 1993). Although discrepancies exist among educators and researchers concerning definitions, processes, goals, and the methods for teaching reading comprehension in school classrooms, virtually all would agree without hesitation that reading comprehension skills are essential to thrive in a world saturated with traditional and digital print.

The National Reading Panel (2000) defined reading comprehension as "*intentional thinking* during which meaning is constructed through interactions between text and reader. . . . The construction of meaning is influenced by the text and by the reader's prior knowledge and experience that are brought to bear on it" (pp. 4–5, emphasis added). The RAND Reading Study Group (Snow, 2002) described the elements of reading comprehension as the following:

1. The reader
2. The text
3. The purpose for reading
4. The sociocultural context shaped by such things as the reader's home environment, peer groups, and relationships within the school setting

The first three components—the reader, the text, and the purpose for reading—occur within the fourth element, the sociocultural context. The *reader* is the one doing the comprehending, and the *text* is the object to be comprehended (literature, informational text, etc.). The *purpose* refers to the kind of task, skill, strategy, or concept the reader is attempting to perform (e.g., determining key ideas and details, following a sequence of events, or thinking about an author's perspective).

The *sociocultural context* of reading comprehension can be thought of in at least two ways. First, sociocultural context is the actual physical setting where reading occurs—at home, in a school classroom, the library, under a blanket with a flashlight at bedtime, and so on. Second, it is the social situation in which the comprehension of what is read occurs. In some cases, reading comprehension occurs individually—when the reader is alone. In other cases, reading comprehension occurs within a vibrant social exchange where students and teachers read a text together and jointly construct and integrate meaning through discussion.

Prior to learning to read, young children's narrative comprehension processes develop in parallel with oral language skills. Young children who possess strong oral language skills and who have the ability to comprehend texts aurally and orally tend to succeed later on in reading comprehension (Kendeou, van den Broek, White, & Lynch, 2007). Research also has shown that young children who struggle to comprehend oral language often struggle as well in early reading instruction and beyond (Catts, Fey, Tomblin, & Zhang, 2002; Kamhi & Catts, 2002; Nation, Cocksey, Taylor, & Bishop, 2010). As a consequence, there is little reason to delay comprehension instruction in the early years of schooling, first as a skill for oral language and then as foundational to print comprehension.

The view that comprehension instruction should and can be taught effectively to students in the early grades differs dramatically from a long-held view that decoding processes must be developed before comprehension processes. The Common Core State Standards endorse comprehension instruction in the early grades, as evidenced in the speaking and listening strand's comprehension Anchor Standard and in the reading strand's first three three clusters—key ideas and details, craft and structure, and integration of knowledge and ideas—of 10 Anchor Standards.

Schema theory, a widely known and popular theory of reading comprehension, for many years informed classroom comprehension instruction (Anderson & Pearson, 1981). Schema theory, in its time, was a quantum leap forward from previous practices that emphasized the teaching of discrete reading comprehension skills. Schema theory emphasized how important a reader's background knowledge was in the process of comprehending text. Schemas are represented as "packages" of knowledge stored in a reader's long-term memory that can be enlisted to aid in the comprehension of text. Schema theory, and its subsequent research, has demonstrated quite convincingly that when students bring copious amounts of background knowledge about language, text, and the world to the task of text comprehension, they have a much easier time making sense of it (Pressley, 2001). Consequently, teachers, even in the earliest years of schooling, can have an observable effect on the development of students' schemas, which are strong enablers of text comprehension.

On the other hand, schema theory, as a framework for teaching reading comprehension, often positioned the text as an obstacle to comprehension that could be overcome by activating or building schemas rather than as an evidentiary base for constructing or elaborating students' schemas. For example, teachers who ground their instruction in schema theory would likely scaffold students' background knowledge for the story of the *Little Red Hen* by focusing on the story's theme and how it connects to the students' background experiences rather than focusing instruction on the text and how to build or elaborate a schema by constructing a mental representation of text-based information.

The effects of anchoring classroom comprehension instruction in schema theory have become ubiquitous in published core reading programs and in observations of teachers' comprehension instructional practices. When schema theory is used to inform comprehension instruction, teachers typically begin a lesson by "activating" or "building" their students' background knowledge as preparation for encountering the text. Because schemas cannot overcome all text obstacles, often students also are taught comprehension strategies as a "stop-gap" for working their way through a text. Discussions around text, when informed by schema theory, often have focused also on responding to or assessing the constellation of ideas students bring to the text from their background knowledge rather than attending predominantly to text-dependent ideas. In short, the context and emphasis that have characterized schema-driven comprehension instruction in elementary classrooms have focused primarily on developing a schema by activating, building, elaborating, or modifying students' background knowledge. An unanticipated outcome of the focus on schema theory and its applications to comprehension instruction in elementary classrooms has been an unintended neglect of text as an evidentiary base for supporting multiple levels of comprehension processing.

With the adoption of the Common Core State Standards (National Governors Association Center for Best Practices [NGA Center] & Council of Chief State School Officers [CCSSO] , 2010) for English Language Arts (ELA), the text, rather than the reader, has been positioned as the focal point of classroom comprehension instruction. With this change, text is to be treated as a rich evidentiary base of knowledge about the world, language, and the content and structure of text itself in the service of reading comprehension.

The CCSS for speaking, listening, and reading have been designed and sequenced to fit a model of text comprehension processes that schema theory does not adequately describe. Furthermore, these standards direct classroom teachers to implement a different focus for comprehension instruction than has been employed in the past (Duke et al., 2011). Before we describe how the CCSS for speaking, listening, and reading require teachers to employ a different theoretical model of comprehension processes to inform their comprehension instruction in classrooms, we thought it might be useful to provide a brief overview of the content and structure of the Common Core Reading Standards. Table 1.1 also shows the close connections between the CI process of comprehension development and the requirements of the CCSS.

BRIEF OVERVIEW OF THE COMMON CORE READING STANDARDS: STRUCTURE AND CONTENT

Although not all U.S. states have adopted the Common Core Reading Standards, it is highly likely that even in those states that have not, the CCSS will have some influence on the writing of state reading standards. States like Texas, which has not adopted the CCSS, also will likely be influenced both by the widespread acceptance of the CCSS across the nation and by published materials purchased and used in schools that respond to the demands of the CCSS.

The CCSS Reading Standards have been organized into three separate substrands: *foundational reading skills, literature,* and *informational text.* Foundational reading skills are intended to focus on developing young students' abilities to recognize words automatically and read connected text fluently. The remaining two reading substrands—literature and informational text—are broken out to highlight a strong focus on reading a balance of different text types. These two substrands of the CCSS Reading Standards are further emphasized by the recommendation

Table 1.1. Connecting Reading CCSS Literature/Informational Text Standards to CI Model Comprehension Process Levels (K–2)

CLUSTER 1: KEY IDEAS AND DETAILS

CI MODEL PROCESSES

Anchor Standards: Literature

1(K): With prompting and support, ask and answer questions about key details in a text.

1(1): Ask and answer questions about key details in a text.

1(2): Ask and answer such questions as who, what, where, when, why, and how to demonstrate understanding of key details in a text.

Anchor Standards: Informational Text

1 (K) With prompting and support, ask, and answer questions about key details in a text.

1 (1) Ask and answer questions about key details in a text.

1 (2) Ask and answer such questions as who, what, where, when, why and how to demonstrate understanding of key details in a text.

Micro Process

Anchor Standards: Literature

2 (K): With prompting and support, retell familiar stories, including key details.

2 (1): Retell stories, including key details, and demonstrate understanding of their central message or lesson.

2 (2): Recount stories, including fables and folktales from diverse cultures, and determine their central message, lesson, or moral.

Anchor Standards: Informational Text

2 (K) With prompting and support, identify the main topic and retell key details of a text.

2 (1) Identify the main topic and retell key details of a text.

2 (2) Identify the main topic of a multiparagraph text as well as the focus of specific paragraphs within the text.

Macro and Micro Process

Anchor Standards: Literature

3 (K): With prompting and support, identify characters, settings, and major events in a story.

3 (1): Describe characters, settings, and major events in a story, using key details.

3 (2): Describe how characters in a story respond to major events and challenges.

Anchor Standards: Informational Text

3 (K): With prompting and support, describe the connection between two individuals, events, ideas, or pieces of information in a text.

3 (1): Describe the connection between two individuals, events, ideas, or pieces of information in a text.

3 (2): Describe the connection between a series of historical events, scientific ideas or concepts, or steps in technical procedures in a text.

Situation Process

Table 1.1. Connecting Reading CCSS Literature/Informational Text Standards to CI Model Comprehension Process Levels (K–2), *continued*

| CLUSTER 2: CRAFT AND STRUCTURE | CI MODEL PROCESSES |

CLUSTER 2: CRAFT AND STRUCTURE

Cluster 2: Anchor Standards: Literature

4 (K): Ask and answer questions about unknown words in a text.

4 (1): Identify words and phrases in stories or poems that suggest feelings or appeal to the senses.

4 (2): Describe how words and phrases (e.g., regular beats, alliteration, rhymes, repeated lines) supply rhythm and meaning in a story, poem, or song.

Anchor Standards: Informational Text

4 (K): With prompting and support, ask and answer questions about unknown words in a text.

4 (1): Ask and answer questions to help determine or clarify the meaning of words and phrases in a text.

4 (2): Determine the meaning of words and phrases in a text relevant to a *grade 2 topic* or *subject area.*

Micro Process

Anchor Standards: Literature

5 (K): Recognize common types of texts (e.g., storybooks, poems).

5 (1): Explain major differences between books that tell stories and books that give information, drawing on a wide reading of a range of text types.

5 (2): Describe the overall structure of a story, including describing how the beginning introduces the story and the ending concludes the action.

Anchor Standards: Informational Text

5 (K): Identify the front cover, back cover, and title page of a book.

5 (1): Know and use various text features (e.g., headings, tables of contents, glossaries, electronic menus, icons) to locate key facts or information in a text.

5 (2): Know and use various text features (e.g., captions, bold print, subheadings, glossaries, indexes, electronic menus, icons) to locate key facts or information in a text efficiently.

Macro Process

Anchor Standards: Literature

6 (K): With prompting and support, name the author and illustrator of a story and define the role of each in telling the story.

6 (1): Identify who is telling the story at various points in a text.

6 (2): Acknowledge differences in the points of view of characters, including by speaking in a different voice for each character when reading dialogue aloud.

Anchor Standards: Informational Text

6 (K): Name the author and illustrator of a text and define the role of each in presenting the ideas or information in a text.

6 (1): Distinguish between information provided by pictures or other illustrations and information provided by the words in a text.

6 (2): Identify the main purpose of a text, including what the author wants to answer, explain, or describe.

Situation Process

Table 1.1. Connecting Reading CCSS Literature/Informational Text Standards to CI Model Comprehension Process Levels (K-2), *continued*

CLUSTER 3: INTEGRATION OF KNOWLEDGE AND IDEAS	CI MODEL PROCESSES

Anchor Standards: Literature

7 (K): With prompting and support, describe the relationship between illustrations and the story in which they appear (e.g., what moment in a story an illustration depicts).

7 (1): Use illustrations and details in a story to describe its characters, setting, or events.

7 (2): Use information gained from the illustrations and words in a print or digital text to demonstrate understanding of its characters, setting, or plot.

Anchor Standards: Informational Text

7 (K): With prompting and support, describe the relationship between illustrations and the text in which they appear (e.g., what person, place, thing, or idea in the text an illustration depicts).

7 (1): Use the illustrations and details in a text to describe its key ideas.

7 (2): Explain how specific images (e.g., a diagram showing how a machine works) contribute to and clarify a text.

> *Situation Process*

Anchor Standards: Literature

8 (K): (RL.K.8 not applicable to literature)

8 (1): (RL.1.8 not applicable to literature)

8 (2): (RL.2.8 not applicable to literature)

Anchor Standards: Informational Text

8 (K): With prompting and support, identify the reasons an author gives to support points in a text.

8 (1): Identify the reasons an author gives to support points in a text.

8 (2): Describe how reasons support specific points the author makes in a text.

Anchor Standards: Literature

9 (K): With prompting and support, compare and contrast the adventures and experiences of characters in familiar stories.

9 (1): Compare and contrast the adventures and experiences of characters in stories.

9 (2): Compare and contrast two or more versions of the same story (e.g., Cinderella stories) by different authors or from different cultures.

Anchor Standards: Informational Text

9 (K): With prompting and support, identify basic similarities in and differences between two texts on the same topic (e.g., in illustrations, descriptions, or procedures).

9 (1): Identify basic similarities in and differences between two texts on the same topic (e.g., in illustrations, descriptions, or procedures).

9 (2): Compare and contrast the most important points presented by two texts on the same topic.

> *World Knowledge Acquisition Process*

that even young students listen to or read a balance (a 50/50 proportion) of informational text and literature.

These two substrands of the CCSS Reading Standards, literature and informational text, are further broken down into four Anchor Standard clusters: (1) *key ideas and details,* (2) *craft and structure,* (3) *integration of knowledge and ideas,* and (4) *range of reading and level of text complexity.* Each of these four Anchor Standard clusters is broken down even further into 10 individual Reading Anchor Standards. Reading Anchor Standards 1–3 are grouped under the key ideas and details cluster; Reading Anchor Standards 4–6 are grouped under the craft and structure cluster; Reading Anchor Standards 7–9 are grouped under the integration of knowledge and ideas cluster; and Standard 10 is under the range of reading and level of text complexity cluster. Each of the 10 Reading Anchor Standards for literature and informational text was designed to result in students who demonstrate college and career readiness. The design of the CCSS originally was conceptualized as a descending learning sequence beginning with 12th-grade literacy competencies necessary for achieving career and college readiness, and descending downward in a staircase-like fashion to kindergarten-level literacy competencies (see Figure 1.1).

Reading Anchor Standards 1–3, under the key ideas and details cluster, highlight the ability to read literature or informational text, determine what the text says, make logical local inferences among ideas represented in the text, and then determine which ideas are key and which ideas support the identified key ideas as details. The express aim of these Reading Standards is to reorient the focus of comprehension instruction toward comprehending text as a rich source of knowledge about language, content, text structure, and the world, to be extracted in the service of reading comprehension and general knowledge acquisition. Reading Anchor Standards 1–3 aim to encourage readers to encounter text as an object of study and to initially construct an accurate and coherent representation of the ideas in the text. Reading Anchor Standards 4–6, under the craft and structure cluster, emphasize the reader's responsibility to make global inferences among key ideas, identify or impose a structure upon the text, note specific word choices, or determine the author's uses of other literary devices in crafting a text. Reading Anchor Standards 7–9, under the integration of knowledge and ideas cluster, involve students in integrating ideas constructed from the text using Standards 1–6 in combination with background knowledge to create a mental model of the ideas represented in the text in order to interpret what the text means.

The CCSS Reading Anchor Standards clearly endorse a text-focused model of comprehension processing. Positioning text as the focal point

Figure 1.1. Design of the Common Core State Standards: English Language Arts (K–12)

	texts	knowledge	thinking	skills
Grade 12				
Grade 11	complex	new	abstract	automatic
Grade 10				
Grade 9				
Grade 8				
Grade 7				
Grade 6				
Grade 5				
Grade 4				
Grade 3				
Grade 2				
Grade 1				
Grade K	simple	known	concrete	effortful and strategic

International Performance Standards as Assessed on the PISA and PIRLS

Common Core Standards ELA Standards Reverse Engineered to Meet International Standards

of comprehension instruction, instead of developing the reader's schemas and frontloading text information, is a significant shift precipitated by the design of the CCSS Reading Standards. In so doing, the design and sequence of the CCSS Reading Anchor Standard clusters—(1) key ideas and details, (2) craft and structure, and (3) integration of knowledge and ideas—invoke both a different model for understanding the process of comprehending a text and an innovative framework for guiding and providing classroom comprehension instruction in classrooms.

When considering which model of text comprehension processing is invoked by the design and sequence of CCSS Reading Anchor Standard clusters 1–3, we have found the Construction–Integration Model of Text Comprehension provides the closest and most logical fit.

The CI Model provides the most complete and fully developed explanation of text comprehension processes currently available (Duke et al., 2011; Graesser, 2007; Pearson & Hiebert, 2015; Wilkinson & Son, 2011). The CI Model supports and informs the design and sequence of the CCSS Reading Anchor Standard clusters by describing text comprehension as a multileveled process (Duke et al., 2011). Just as understanding schema theory helped to propel classroom teachers' comprehension instruction forward over the past 3 decades, teachers can benefit greatly from gaining a knowledge and understanding of the CI Model of Text Comprehension to inform and foreground their use of the CCSS Reading Anchor Standards as the basis for their current and future classroom reading comprehension instruction.

THE CONSTRUCTION-INTEGRATION MODEL OF TEXT COMPREHENSION

The CI Model describes two processes through which readers comprehend text: *construction* and *integration*. At the outset of our description of the CI Model, we want to make clear that in proficient, adult readers, the twin comprehension processes of construction and integration are automatic, whereas in younger, less proficient readers, they are effortful and strategic. Also, because the CI Model uses terms that may be relatively unfamiliar to readers, we have created a list of these terms with their definitions:

- *Construction*—The process of combining information available in a text at the micro- and macrostructure levels to construct or create an internal representation of the meaning of a text.
- *Integration*—The process of relating the meaning constructed from reading a text to experiences with other texts and in life.
- *Macrostructure*—The features, words, and phrases found in text that signal how texts are organized, including glossaries, headings, graphics, photos, tables of contents, figures, indexes in informational texts, and foreshadowing and flashbacks in narrative texts.
- *Microstructure*—The meanings of words, phrases, and sentences, and linking or connector terms between and among sentences, i.e., ordinal, causal, and temporal connector terms like first, because, and after. This also includes words and phrases that authors use to craft texts that are engaging, descriptive, and rich with imagery

and linguistic devices, such as metaphors, similes, and figurative language.

- *Situation model*—The reader's understanding and interpretation of the meaning of the text in light of the individual's background knowledge of the world and of other texts. In other words, comprehension of the text is "situated" within readers' broader knowledge and is constrained by the contents and organization of the text both of which inform future encounters with other texts and experiences.

- *Textbase*—The product of the process of text construction at the micro and macro levels. This is a representation of the constructed meaning contained in and constrained by the content and structure of the original text.

To begin our description of the CI Model, the construction process involves two levels of text-based comprehension processing: (1) *microstructure* and (2) *macrostructure*. The combination of these two levels of text comprehension processes results in the creation or construction of something called a *textbase*. A textbase is a representational model of the text constructed in the reader's mind. It represents the ideas and the connections among ideas as conveyed by the words, phrases, and sentences in the text and as assisted by the reader's word-meaning and linguistic background knowledge. In essence, the textbase, when properly constructed, should represent what the text actually says.

The integration process, as described in the CI Model, involves integrating information from the constructed *textbase* with the contents of the reader's world network of background knowledge to create a *situation model* of the text. A situation model is more than what the text says; it is what the text means to the reader.

To illustrate how the two CI processes, construction and integration, work, we describe what goes on inside the mind of a young reader. In so doing, we hope teachers of young children can understand and appreciate the complex, multileveled processes that permit comprehension of text. We begin our description with the first level of the CI Model's description of comprehension processes, construction.

Caution: Microstructure Construction Ahead!

Nina is a 1st-grade student who is reading an information book titled *Sand* (Clyne & Griffiths, 2005). As she picks up the book to read, she is immediately confronted with a complex perceptual and decoding task. She must be able to recognize the illustrations and symbols on the pages of the text and decode or recognize what the symbols, words, and illustrations represent (e.g., sand, rock, wind, rain, waves, deserts, dunes, beaches, etc.).

Once decoded, the words, phrases, and sentences are placed into Nina's working memory. Through the process of construction, Nina links the decoded words, phrases, and sentences in working memory to word meanings and to images or experiences stored in her background knowledge. Next, she places the constructed meanings for words, phrases, and sentences in the text into a running list of related propositions or ideas meaningfully linked together in her working memory, called a microstructure (Perfetti & Stafura, 2014).

For example, in the book *Sand,* Nina reads the first sentence, *What is sand?* To begin, ideally Nina decodes each word in this sentence accurately and effortlessly, leaving sufficient cognitive resources available to focus on constructing a microstructure of what the text actually says. As each word in the sentence is decoded and entered into Nina's working memory, it is then associated with a meaning.

> *What* . . . a word used to ask a question about a person, place, thing, or idea (noun) . . .
> *is* . . . a verb indicating a state of being or existence . . .
> *sand* . . . an object like dirt, but found at the beach or in boxes at the local city park.

As this process proceeds, assisted by knowledge of word meanings and linguistic knowledge about sentence structure, Nina begins to construct a mental model of the microstructure of the text or what the text actually says.

The next sentence in the book reads, *Sand is many tiny pieces of rock.* As the words in this second sentence are decoded and associated with word meanings stored in our Nina's word-meaning and linguistic knowledge base of sentence structures, links are formed in her mind between the word meanings in this sentence (*many, tiny, pieces,* and *rock*) and the concept of *sand* in the first sentence. As newly decoded words in the text are linked to word meanings stored in Nina's background knowledge, she continues to construct the meaning of the microstructure of the text, or what the words, phrases, sentences, and inter-sentence linking or connector terms in the text actually mean (see Figure 1.2).

Figure 1.2. C-I Model of Text Comprehension: Constructing the Microstructure of Text

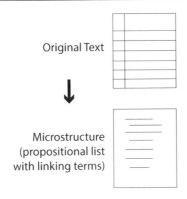

Original Text

Microstructure
(propositional list
with linking terms)

Younger, less proficient readers often need to be helped to establish coherence at the local level of text comprehension—words, phrases, sentences, and paragraphs. Authors can help by providing cohesion connectors or signal words in the text. Cohesion terms or signal words like *next, so, and,* and *because* help readers explicitly link one idea to others contained in a string of propositions or meaningful idea units in the text. For example, the word *similarly* in a sentence signals that ideas to come in a new proposition are to be linked with ideas in previous propositions. Or the word *because* in a sentence signals that ideas in one sentence often link to ideas in a second sentence in a chain of cause and effect. When authors omit cohesion terms or signal words, readers, like our 1st-grader Nina, must infer or impose relationships upon the ideas represented in text (Pearson, 1974).

After Nina turns the page in the *Sand* text, the next sentence reads, *How is sand made?* The text continues:

Wind blows on rocks.
Rain falls on rocks.
Waves crash on rocks.
The wind, rain, and waves break the rock into tiny pieces.
The rock becomes sand.

Similar to the processes already described above, the microstructure of the text constructed in Nina's mind continues to grow with input from the text as she consults her word-meaning dictionary (lexicon) and her linguistic background knowledge about sentence structure and cohesion terms.

Caution: Macrostructure Construction Ahead!

As Nina's reading of the *Sand* text continues, her teacher might point out to her that each new paragraph in this particular information text begins with a question and then each question is answered with a series of statements. With this information provided by her teacher, Nina is enabled to construct a coherent mental model or organized representation of the *Sand* text at a global level, called a macrostructure. Her teacher helped her to recognize hierarchical relationships among various key ideas in the text to highlight a particular organizational pattern or text structure. In the case of the *Sand* text this text structure was question–answer.

When authors organize the ideas in texts using identifiable text structure(s), it makes the construction of a globally coherent model or organized representation of meaning in the text, the macrostructure, much easier. Conversely, when authors fail to organize text using clearly identifiable text structures, readers must infer or impose a structure on the ideas extracted from the text to be able to construct a macrostructure (Graesser, 2007; Kintsch, 2013; Kintsch & Kintsch, 2005). When the microstructure (text ideas drawn from propositions and signal terms) and the macrostructure (text understandings drawn from text features, structure, and literary devices) combine, they form something Kintsch (2013) calls a textbase, as shown in Figure 1.3.

Kintsch (2013) explains, "Cooperative and attentive readers will more or less form the same textbase—*micro-* and *macrostructures*—as invited by the author of the text" (p. 811, emphasis added). Once *micro-* and *macrostructures* are merged to complete the construction of a thorough and well-organized textbase, the next level of processing described in the CI Model comes into play: *integration*.

Integration: What's the Situation Here?

Integration involves combining the ideas contained in the textbase with the network of world knowledge stored in a reader's background to form a situation model. A situation model amounts to a reader's mental representation or interpretation of the situation or what is going on as described in the text. This integration happens functionally when the constructed textbase is "situated" or nested within the reader's background knowledge. In the text *Sand,* Nina forms a situation model of the text by linking the content, ideas, connections, and organization represented in the textbase, which was constructed from the original or actual *Sand* text, to content, ideas, or experiences stored in her network of world

Figure 1.3. C-I Model of Text Comprehension: Constructing Macrostructure and Combining It with Microstructure to Construct the Textbase

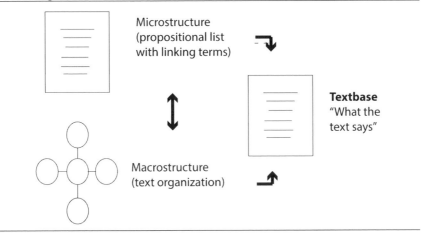

Microstructure
(propositional list
with linking terms)

Textbase
"What the
text says"

Macrostructure
(text organization)

knowledge about sand. For example, she may link the contents of the textbase she constructed from the *Sand* text to her personal experiences with sand—such as being buried in sand at the beach, building sandcastles, or her mother's use of a minute sand glass to poach an egg. When Nina integrates ideas represented in the textbase with her own network of world and experiential background knowledge, she creates a *situation model* or interpretation of the text (see Figure 1.4).

Because each situation model is a composite of information constructed from the textbase and information stored in a reader's network of background knowledge and experiences, it often results in an interpretation of text that is somewhat different from the original text and from that of other students' interpretations. Thus, when a reader creates a situation model, it is different from either what was said in the text or what is stored in a reader's background knowledge. Instead, it is a product of the integration of background knowledge with text-based information to create an interpretation of what the text means or at least what the reader interprets the situation represented in the text to mean. Thus, the integration process by which readers form a situation model is greatly dependent on each reader's abilities to do the following:

1. Construct an accurate and coherent textbase from the original text
2. Access and integrate background knowledge and prior experiences with information in the constructed textbase
3. Make inferences to fill in gaps among the ideas provided by the author

**Figure 1.4. C-I Model of Text Comprehension: Integrating the Textbase with Readers'
Prior Knowledge (Level 1) to Form the Situation Model of Text**

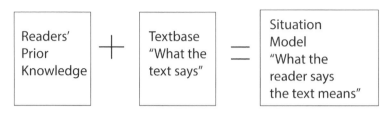

Consequently, it is very difficult to predict with absolute certainty the situation models individual readers may create due to their unique background knowledge, prior experiences, and the inferences they may make as a result. This is not, however, to suggest that the creation of a situation model can be anything the reader wants it to be.

To form a satisfactory situation model, Duke et al. (2011) assert that it must conform to two important constraints. First, the situation model must be consistent with the ideas represented in the textbase. Second, the situation model must correspond to the way the reader views the world through the lens of his/her background knowledge and prior experience. As a consequence, a situation model does not represent so much what the text actually says as much as what the reader has determined the text to mean (see Figure 1.4). Duke et al. (2011) explain, "If the *textbase* is an account of what the text says, then the *situation model* can be thought of as an account of what the text means" (p. 54, emphasis added).

As a result, Nina's situation model of the *Sand* text will likely contain more than an accurate representation that links and organizes the ideas in the textbase. For example, Nina's situation model may contain a collage of images gathered from charts, graphs, photos, or diagrams in the text, combined with images and experiences drawn from her background knowledge and prior experiences with sand. The content of the situation model also will likely reflect her purposes and goals for reading. If her goal for reading the *Sand* text was to answer a set of specific questions, then the situation model she forms might include only information pertinent for answering these questions. On the other hand, if her goal or purpose was to share what she learned with her peers in an oral report or presentation, her situation model might be more inclusive of key ideas and details in the text, the way in which those ideas were organized, as well as related images provided in the text and other connections she brought to the text from her background knowledge, all of which she could employ to share her text understandings with others.

The creation of a situation model from text is often what teachers are most interested in when they assess their students' reading comprehension. Most teachers are not very interested in whether students can recite the words or sentences in a text verbatim. Rather, they are more interested in whether students can describe a satisfactory situation model that makes sense in relation to the parameters dictated by the text and the connections made to their background knowledge, prior experiences, and information learned from other, related texts.

Integrating the Situation Model into Background Knowledge

Creating a situation model of the text does not, however, complete the integration process as described in the CI Model of Text Comprehension (Kintsch, 2013). To complete the integration process, readers must integrate the contents of the situation model held in working memory into their world knowledge network stored in long-term memory (see Figure 1.5).

So now that Nina has formed a situation model of the *Sand* text that includes answers to several questions, such as What is sand? How is sand made? Where is sand found? and What things are made with sand? she will next need to be helped to take conscious, active steps to integrate the contents of her situation model of the *Sand* text into her network of world knowledge. To do this, Nina may consciously link the concept of sand as a specialized type of soil or dirt to her background knowledge because she has had more experiences with dirt than with sand. She may, with help from her teacher, use a Venn diagram to compare and contrast sand with dirt—how dirt and sand are made, where dirt and sand are found, and things that can be made with dirt and sand. This conscious, effortful linking of known world knowledge about dirt (stored in long-term memory) with new knowledge about sand from the *Sand* text (held in working memory) is necessary for younger, less fluent readers—and even some more accomplished readers—to transfer the contents of a situation model into their world knowledge network stored in long-term memory.

Kintsch (2013) cautions that failure to help students consciously and actively integrate the contents of their situation models into the related network of their global or world knowledge can result in what is called *encapsulated knowledge*. Encapsulated knowledge can be retrieved only by employing cues from a particular text. In other words, encapsulated knowledge is not consciously generalized, transferred, or integrated into the world knowledge network of the reader. As such, encapsulated

Figure 1.5. C-I Model of Text Comprehension – Integrating the Situation Model (Level 2) into the Readers' Global and World Knowledge

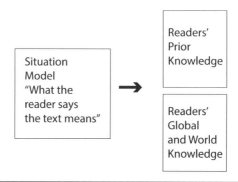

knowledge remains linked to a single text or situation model, and remains isolated from the contents of the reader's world knowledge network.

Imagine that Nina, or her teacher, had made no efforts to transfer the contents of her situation model into her world knowledge network after reading the *Sand* text. Then, imagine a friend later on asked Nina whether she had ever been to a beach. Without the contents of the "sand" situation model integrated into her world knowledge base, the question asked might not contain sufficient cues to link to the situation model contents of the *Sand* text, her experiences at a beach, so that Nina could retrieve it from her long-term memory to answer the question. This would constitute encapsulated knowledge of the *Sand* text. On the other hand, if Nina had engaged in integrating the contents of her situation model into her world knowledge network, as we described previously, she might respond by retrieving the related information learned about beaches as found in the *Sand* text or her own experiences at a beach. Encapsulated knowledge represents an incomplete text comprehension process where the virtuous cycle of comprehension described by Duke et al. (2011)—knowledge begets comprehension begets knowledge—is disrupted.

Integrating the information contained in the situation model into information stored in the world knowledge base is quite typical of adult, fluent readers, but it is not an automatic process to be assumed with younger, less fluent readers. According to Kintsch (2013), integration of the contents of a situation model into one's world knowledge network stored in long-term memory requires "strategic action and effort on the part of the reader/learner" (p. 812). To integrate the contents of a situation model into world knowledge, younger (and struggling) readers must actively integrate new knowledge into old, often consciously employing a variety of comprehension strategies, including text discussion with others, to do so. Figure 1.6 represents the complete CI text comprehension model with its two major components labeled—construction and integration—showing how text comprehension is composed of multiple levels of comprehension processing.

As shown in Figure 1.6 and by way of a quick review, text processing begins with a text to be read. First, the text to be read must be perceived and decoded by the reader. Second, proficient readers construct an accurate mental representation linking the ideas in the text together, called a microstructure. Simultaneously or sometimes during a subsequent reading, skilled readers identify how the author organizes or imposes a global organization upon the hierarchical relations among ideas represented in the text, called a macrostructure. When microstructure and macrostructure are combined in working memory, the result is the construction of a textbase or an accurate, organized, locally (phrase, sentence, paragraph) and globally (discourse, text structure) coherent representation of what the text actually said. Poor readers sometimes will insert information from their background knowledge that does not fit with information in the text. Consequently, the contents in the textbase provide an important constraint upon a reader's construction of meaning—readers must construct meaning using the ideas represented in the text.

After a textbase has been constructed, it is integrated (see Figure 1.4) with a reader's network of world knowledge and prior experiences and held in working memory to create a situation model of the text—what the reader interprets the text to mean. Finally, proficient readers often actively integrate the contents of their situation models into their world knowledge network stored in long-term memory to learn and acquire knowledge. When this happens, as it should, the virtuous comprehension cycle functions as it should: A proficient reader's *knowledge begets comprehension and comprehension begets new knowledge*!

Kintsch (1998) originally described what fluent, adult readers do to process text. In a later update of the CI Model, he stated that beginning readers will need to use conscious cognitive effort, affective engagement, and active processing in order to develop over time into fluent, adult readers (Kintsch, 2013). Kintsch and Kintsch (2005) have rebuffed arguments suggesting that the CI Model cannot be used to explain the text comprehension of younger students. They claim it is precisely by understanding the striking contrast between novice readers' reading comprehension processes and those of fluent, adult readers, that teachers and

Figure 1.6. Total C-I Model of Text Comprehension: Virtuous Cycle

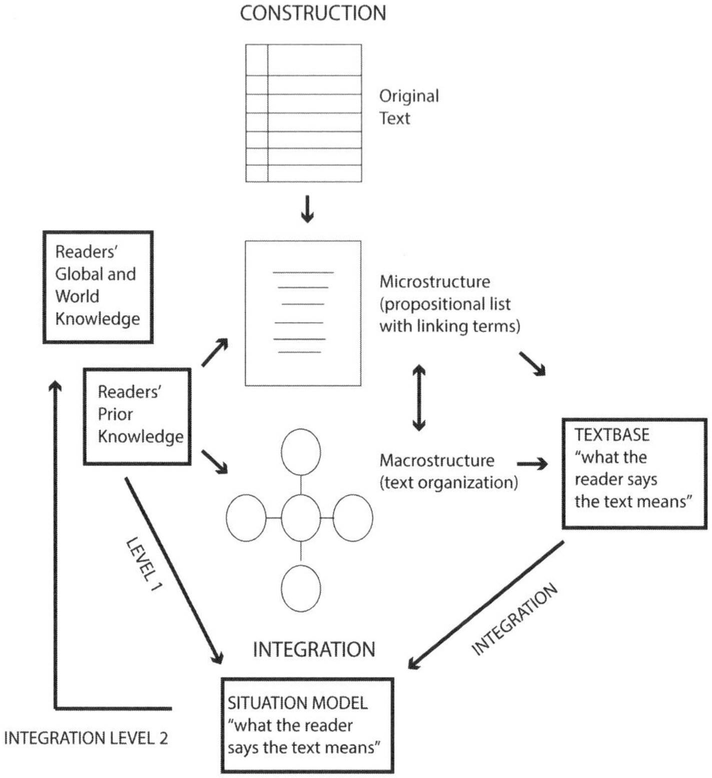

CONSTRUCTION

Original Text

Readers' Global and World Knowledge

Microstructure (propositional list with linking terms)

Readers' Prior Knowledge

Macrostructure (text organization)

TEXTBASE "what the reader says the text means"

LEVEL 1

INTEGRATION

INTEGRATION

INTEGRATION LEVEL 2

SITUATION MODEL "what the reader says the text means"

curriculum designers can better conceptualize transformative comprehension instruction that will accommodate readers' instructional needs across a wide developmental span (Kintsch & Kintsch, 2005). Although Kintsch's (1998) initial model of text comprehension analyzed relatively small units of text, recent updates to the CI Model have focused on explaining how readers process longer units of text (discourse level), as well as considerations related to different text genres, readers' goals and purposes, and so on.

Teachers who understand the CI Model of Text Comprehension are better equipped to support their students' multileveled text comprehension processes through well-planned and sequenced discussion and strategy instruction using text as an evidentiary base for constructing and integrating text-based information to form a situation model of text rather than an over-reliance on teacher frontloading of text information.

Conversely, teachers with limited theoretical understandings of the CI Model will likely continue to provide comprehension instruction largely foregrounded by schema theory, replete with well-intentioned, but often excessive, frontloading of text-based information and unintentionally undercutting students' opportunities to develop independence in text comprehension processes. Continuing to focus comprehension instruction on activating and building the reader's schema prior to encountering the text, rather than teaching and modeling how specific comprehension strategies can be used during reading to independently construct and integrate meaning from text to acquire knowledge and learn independently, simply isn't in the best long-term interests of our students. Kucan, Hapgood, and Palincsar (2011) appropriately have asserted that "recent models of text comprehension and text analysis are important aspects of the specialized knowledge that teachers need in order to think about a text in ways that will allow them to support their students in making sense of it" (p. 78). This is particularly true when using CCSS Reading Standards to teach younger students to comprehend challenging texts at multiple levels of comprehension. In the next section of this chapter, we answer several questions about how the alignment of the CI Model with CCSS Reading Standards will promote significant shifts in teachers' classroom comprehension instructional content, sequence, and practices. We begin by answering the question about the way in which theoretical knowledge of the CI Model can make a difference in how reading comprehension will be taught in classrooms using the CCSS Reading Standards.

As discussed earlier, reading comprehension instruction in many classrooms has been powerfully influenced by teachers' theoretical understandings of schema theory. A shift away from schema theory toward comprehension instruction, guided by a CI Model of text comprehension processes, necessitates significant shifts in how classroom teachers conceptualize and implement comprehension instruction. Before making such significant shifts, classroom teachers deserve answers to two questions: First, why should they change to a CI Model of text comprehension to inform comprehension instruction? Second, what will changes look like as they make this shift to comprehension instruction informed by a CI Model of text comprehension?

FOUR REASONS TO SWITCH TO THE CI MODEL OF
TEXT COMPREHENSION

We have identified at least four advantages for teachers' changing from comprehension instruction informed by schema theory to comprehension instruction informed by the CI Model of Text Comprehension:

1. Although schema theory and the CI Model share a lot in common, the CI Model is recognized as the more complete and fully developed explanation of how readers actually go about the task of learning from text (Duke et al., 2011). Relying on an older, less well-developed model of comprehension processes to inform the design of comprehension instruction today, when a better, more fully developed model exists, isn't in the best interests of either teachers or students.

2. The CI Model positions the text and text processing, rather than the reader and schema development, as the focal point of comprehension instruction. The text is viewed as a rich evidentiary base to be used to support multileveled comprehension processing. This includes a balanced focus on the genres of texts to be read—literature and informational text.

3. The CI Model represents text comprehension as a multileveled process, which closely aligns with similarly sequenced CCSS Reading Anchor Standard clusters. Viewing text comprehension as a multileveled process invokes a new framework for comprehension instruction that develops students' abilities to engage text at multiple levels of comprehension processing.

4. Instruction that develops students' abilities to engage text at multiple levels of comprehension processing, as represented in the CI Model, strongly suggests that teachers will do the following:

   » Select multiple standards rather than a single standard for teaching comprehension of a single text
   » Teach students to use multiple sets of comprehension strategies specifically selected to target the unique demands of each level of text comprehension processing
   » Employ multiple "close readings" (defined below) of text to support students' movement through text at multiple levels of comprehension processing

WHAT WILL CHANGES LOOK LIKE?

The CI Model positions text and its content and structure at the initial levels of text comprehension processing—*construction of a textbase.* Although word-meaning and linguistic background knowledge is acknowledged to play a role in the initial levels of text comprehension processing in the CI Model, it plays an assistive role rather than the central role.

Similarly, schema theory described comprehension as a unitary rather than a multileveled process. Consequently, comprehension strategies often were taught one at a time or in a single set of multiple strategies targeted to the entire or unitary comprehension process (Duke, 2005). When the CI Model informs comprehension instruction, it treats comprehension as a multileveled process rather than a unitary or single process. As a result, multiple and flexible sets of comprehension strategies are taught as cognitive tools to be used strategically to respond to the text-processing demands encountered at each of several levels of comprehension. For example:

- In the initial levels of text processing, students are taught to use a set of specific comprehension strategies, such as paraphrasing, sentence combining, and recognizing signal or cohesion terms, to aid them in construction of a microstructure of text or what the text actually says.
- Later on at a different level of text comprehension, where the textbase has been constructed and is ready to be integrated with the reader's network of world knowledge to form a situation model of the text, students may be instructed to use a set of discussion or dialogic strategies to assist them.
- Finally, once a situation model of the text has been created, yet another set of comprehension strategies, such as retelling, summarizing, and presenting, are taught to help readers take active steps to integrate the contents of their situation models into their world knowledge networks.

Consequently, when comprehension strategy instruction is foregrounded by the CI Model, comprehension strategy selection and instruction are nuanced to support each of several levels of text comprehension processing as part of the construction of a textbase and integration of world knowledge and textbase knowledge to create a situation model.

Another significant change in comprehension instruction supported by a CI Model has to do with the number of readings of a text. Schema theory treated reading comprehension as a unitary process, so texts typically were read only once. On the other hand, because the CI Model treats text comprehension as a multileveled process, rereadings of text, called "close readings," often are necessitated in order to comprehend texts at multiple levels. Cummins (2013) and Fisher and Frey (2012) define close reading as analyzing a text to make a determination about which ideas are most important and how these ideas fit together logically to convey an author's central topic or message.

Discussions of text, informed by schema theory, focused comprehension instruction on assessing students' interpretations of text, along with a strong emphasis on how background knowledge shaped their text interpretations. On the other hand, text discussions supported by the CI Model focus on helping students to construct what the text says and then integrate text-based information with their world knowledge network to create a situation model, interpretation of, or meaning of the text. An adequate situation model of text cannot be achieved when personal connections to prior knowledge are privileged over the processes of constructing a textbase from the evidence in the text and then integrating text-based knowledge with the reader's network of world knowledge and prior experiences.

Another change necessitated by the shift from schema theory to comprehension instruction informed by a CI Model is how teachers select and use standards. Because comprehension was viewed as a unitary process in the past, many teachers and core reading instructional programs selected a single objective or standard on which to focus their comprehension instruction. As teachers come to view text comprehension as a multileveled process that results in the acquisition and retention of text-based knowledge, they also will want to select and sequence multiple reading standards to specifically address and match up with each level of a multileveled text comprehension process.

For example, teachers may select an individual Reading Anchor Standard from within those grouped under the first CCSS Reading Anchor Standard cluster—determining key ideas and details—to address the CI Model's initial level of text processing, constructing a microstructure of the text. In order to support students' text comprehension processes at the next level of the CI Model, constructing a macrostructure of the text, teachers might select an individual Reading Anchor Standard from those grouped under the second CCSS Reading Anchor Standard cluster—craft and structure. In practice, teaching comprehension lessons that employ multiple or several standards will also require multiple readings of a selected text or close readings in order to support multiple levels of text comprehension processing. In Figure 1.7, we contrast the shifts between reading comprehension lesson elements informed by schema theory and those foregrounded by the CI Model of Text Comprehension.

CONNECTING CI COMPREHENSION INSTRUCTION AND READING STANDARDS

Comprehension instruction informed by knowledge of the CI Model of Text Comprehension precipitates substantial shifts in the ways that teachers implement and young children experience reading comprehension instruction in the CCSS era. In Table 1.2, we show a CI Model–informed instructional framework that captures and organizes the multiple elements of comprehension instruction necessary to emphasize multiple levels of text comprehension processing as represented in the CI Model.

This new instructional framework shows how shifts in comprehension instruction as informed by the CI Model's multiple levels of text comprehension processing relate to the CCSS Reading Anchor Standard clusters. In the first column, we show the levels of text comprehension processing represented in the CI Model. In the second column, we show the CCSS Reading Anchor Standard clusters that relate to the levels of text comprehension processing represented in the CI Model, along with individual Reading Anchor Standards that support the teaching of each CCSS Anchor Standard cluster. In the third column, we show comprehension strategies that can be grouped into a set of strategies to be taught and used to support teaching the cluster of Reading Anchor Standards at each level of the CI Model's text comprehension processes. For teachers to understand how to use this new instructional framework, we describe each of the components of the CI framework along with the CCSS Reading Anchor Category Cluster and numbered Anchor Standards and evidence-based comprehension strategies to be selected as part of instructional decision making as pictured in Table 1.2. This is followed by an illustration of how this framework could be used to design a comprehension lesson for reading an informational text in 1st grade.

Figure 1.7. Contrasting Lesson Elements of Schema Theory and CI Model Comprehension Instruction

Schema Theory–Informed Comprehension Instruction: Lesson Events

- Select a book at the instructional level of text.
- Activate or build background knowledge.
- Provide instruction in a single strategy or a single set of multiple strategies.
- Establish a purpose for reading.
- Admonish students to use background knowledge and comprehension strategies during reading text.
- Require a single reading of a text.
- Conduct teacher-led discussion, sometimes during but more often after reading, using a series of schemas and text-based questions to assess comprehension as a unitary process.

CI Model–Informed Comprehension Instruction: Lesson Events

- Select an appropriately challenging and complex literature or informational text.
- Support the CI Model's first level of text comprehension by selecting CCSS Anchor Standard 1, determining key ideas and details.
- Select a set of multiple comprehension strategies to be taught as tools to aid in the construction of the microstructure level of text.
- Remind students to use their background knowledge where it is helpful at this first level of comprehension processing.
- Support the CI Model's next level of text comprehension by selecting CCSS Anchor Standard 2, craft and structure.
- Select another set of multiple comprehension strategies to be taught as tools to aid in the construction of the macrostructure level of text and the completion of the textbase.
- Remind students during the close reading to use their background knowledge where it is helpful.
- With teacher guidance, have students "close read" the text again to address the next level of text comprehension—macrostructure and textbase construction.
- Support the CI Model's final level of text comprehension by selecting Anchor Standard 3—integration of knowledge and ideas.
- Select another set of comprehension strategies to help students create a situation model or an interpretation of what the text means.
- With guidance from the teacher, have students take active steps to integrate the contents of their situation models into their world background knowledge network by selecting and using yet another set of multiple comprehension strategies, such as summarizing, written responses, presentations, etc.

Selecting a Text

In some cases, publishers do the job of text selection for teachers—as is the case in most core reading programs. In all other cases, the opportunity to select an appropriately challenging, engaging, and supportive text for designing effective comprehension instruction falls on the teacher. The process of selecting a text directly addresses the intent of Reading Anchor Standard cluster 4 and individual Reading Anchor Standard 10—range of reading and level of text complexity. When selecting a text to support effective reading comprehension instruction, teachers must consider four important indicators:

1. The reader–text match
2. The quantitative level of difficulty
3. The qualitative obstacles to comprehension at each level of text comprehension processing
4. The strategies to be employed at each level of text comprehension processing represented in the CI Model

The first order of business is to consider the topic or theme of the text to be read and whether it is likely to be of interest to students. Many teachers assess their students' reading interests using reading interest inventories. Interest in a text is especially important if the text selected is to be read more than once using close readings. Not all texts are worth repeatedly reading for close readings or for any other purpose. Teachers need to be certain the texts selected for comprehension instruction are worthy of multiple close readings for multiple comprehension instruction purposes and are relatively brief.

Next, teachers select a text using the *Goldilocks principle*—a challenge level that is just right. To do this, teachers may begin by examining texts for grade-level difficulty using indicators such as Lexiles®. It is important to select texts that are within the Lexile level "stretch" bandwidth suggested by the CCSS to get at the level of challenge that is just right. Teachers can look up specific book titles at www.lexile.com/fab/ to find the text difficulty levels of the books they are considering (see also www.lexile.com/using-lexile/lexile-measures-and-the-ccssi/text-complexity-grade-bands-and-lexile-ranges/).

After this, teachers also may consider the genre of text to be selected for reading comprehension instruction. If the previous text read by students in the class was a narrative, the next text could be selected from the

Table 1.2. Connections Among CI Model of Text Comprehension, CCSS Reading Standards, and Instructional Decision Making

Construction Integration of Text Comprehension	CCSS Reading Anchor Standard Category/Cluster and Standard Number	Instructional Decision-Making (Evidence-Based Practices)
	10	**Select Text Genre and Complexity Level**: Literature/informational text / Lexile level
Microstructure → ↓	*Key Ideas and Details* →	*Size of Text Unit Focus (Words, Phrases, Sentences)*
	4	**Vocabulary Words** Tier 2 and 3 words
	3, 5	**Establishing Local Text Coherence** Cohesion terms / Vertical structuring of phrases and sentences
	1–5	**Strategy Instruction** Paraphrasing / Graphic organizer / Monitoring / Fix ups
	1, 2	**Discussion/Interaction** Questioning / Retelling / Dramatization
	1–5	**Background Knowledge** Activate / Build / Modify
Macrostructure → ↓	*Craft and Structure* →	*Size of Text Unit Focus (paragraphs, sections, chapters, whole texts)*
	5, 6	**Establishing Global Text Coherence** Literary devices / Text features / Text structure
	5, 6	**Strategy Instruction** Text structure / Graphic organizer / Summarization / Monitoring / Fix ups
	5, 6	**Discussion/Interaction** Close reading / Questions / Retelling / Dramatization

Table 1.2. *Continued*

Construction Integration of Text Comprehension	CCSS Reading Anchor Standard Category/Cluster and Standard Number	Instructional Decision-Making (Evidence-Based Practices)
	5, 6	**Background Knowledge** Activate Build Modify
Integration: Creating a Situation Model of Text ⟶ ↓	*Integration of Knowledge and Ideas*	*Size of Text Unit Focus (Whole Text)*
	7–8	**Discussion** Close reading Questioning Retelling
Integration: Linking the Situation Model with World Knowledge ⟶		*Size of Text Unit Focus (Multiple texts)*
	9	**Strategy Instruction** Graphic organizer Text structure Summarization Presentation Written responses Visuals/illustrations

informational text genre to maintain the CCSS suggested proportion of 50/50 literature to informational texts. This is particularly true if teachers want to maintain a theme or topic across text genres and foster students' intertextual knowledge connections.

Finally, teachers carefully read the text to determine qualitative aspects of the text that may prove to be challenging for students. Such aspects include, but are not limited to, the absence of explicit connecting and signal words; of text features such as headings, illustrations, photos, or a glossary; or of a clearly identifiable text structure. Texts that require students to infer from or impose these qualitative aspects on a text are more challenging than those texts in which authors provide these. As Shanahan (2014) reminds us, teachers should remember that "the point [of text selection] shouldn't be to place students in books easy enough to ensure good reading, but to provide enough scaffolding to allow them to read harder books successfully" (p. 15).

Planning Comprehension Instruction

Effective reading comprehension requires readers to use multiple cognitive processes at multiple levels of text processing, as illustrated in the CI Model of Text Comprehension. In similar fashion, effective reading comprehension instruction engages students in using multiple cognitive processes at several levels of text processing.

Because successful text comprehension begins with the construction of a textbase (micro- and macrostructures) and proceeds to integration in order to create a situation model or an interpretation of what the text means, CCSS Reading Anchor Standard clusters and individual Reading Anchor Standards 1–9 ought to be selected and ordered into a process-driven sequence to support comprehension processing at deeper and deeper levels of meaning. In practice, this means that comprehension instruction informed by a CI Model would begin by selecting Reading Anchor Standards from within the multiple levels of the CCSS Reading Anchor Standard clusters. The three reading standard clusters and the individually numbered Reading Anchor Standards selected for instruction then would be arranged in an ascending sequence from low to high levels of comprehension processes as described in the CI Model. So, rather than selecting a single Reading Anchor Standard to support text comprehension instruction as in the past, teachers who possess theoretical knowledge of the CI Model would select several individual Reading Anchor Standards 1–3 from within cluster 1—key ideas and details; individual Reading Anchor Standards 4–6 from within cluster 2—author's craft and structure; and Reading Anchor Standards 7–9 from within cluster 3—integrating information and ideas, to plan comprehension lessons that support multiple levels of text processing and close readings of text.

The CI Model's multiple levels of text processing then would be deliberately linked, in a somewhat sequential process, to the three CCSS Reading Anchor Standard clusters, which in turn relate to selection of individual Reading Anchor Standards within these standard clusters as shown in the Table 1.1. Therefore, teachers start standard selection within Reading Anchor Standard cluster 1—key ideas and details. Then they select one or more individual Reading Anchor Standards (1–3) to teach within this cluster, such as Anchor Standard 2, shown below, to support the initial level of text comprehension processing—constructing microstructure.

2. Identify the main topic and retell key details of a text.

Next, teachers select another individual Reading Anchor Standard (4–6) from those listed within cluster 2—craft and structure. For example, teachers might select Reading Anchor Standard 5, as shown below, to support the next level of text processing, constructing macrostructure. A subsequent close reading of the text may ensue to determine how the author has used text features to signal text genre and text structure.

5. Know and use various text features (e.g., headings, tables of contents, glossaries, electronic menus, icons) to locate key facts or information in a text.

Finally, teachers might select individual Reading Anchor Standard 7, as shown below, which is listed under the third cluster—integration of knowledge and ideas.

7. Use the illustrations and details in a text to describe its key ideas.

The selection of Standard 7 is intended to support instruction that addresses the final level of CI Model text processing, integration to create a situation model. Standard 7 requires students to explain how illustrations in text inform the reader's understanding of text-based information, and vice versa. Integrating information represented in the illustrations, the textbase, and the reader's background knowledge through focused discussion can help students to create a situation model of the text. Integration, the final level of text processing, may or may not require additional close readings of the text. An additional Anchor Standard can be selected from the integration of knowledge and ideas cluster (Standards 7–9) to help students integrate their situation model of the text into their background knowledge to complete the comprehension cycle.

COMPREHENSION: A CLASSROOM ILLUSTRATION

Our 1st-grade teacher, Ms. Chang, begins her instructional planning by selecting CCSS Reading Anchor Standard cluster 4 (Standard 10) to guide the process of selecting an appropriately challenging and complex text. It is the winter of the academic year and Ms. Chang has been teaching this group of 1st-grade students for nearly 6 months. The most recently read text in her 1st-grade classroom was selected from the literature genre—*Curious George Goes to a Chocolate Factory* (Rey, 1998). Consequently, she selects the next text to be read from the informational text genre to balance her students' exposure to literature and informational text. She decides that she can maximize motivation by looking for an informational text that relates to the topic or theme of the last book they read, chocolate, a tasty topic to be sure! After searching in her school's central book room, she locates an informational text by R. Nelson titled *From Cocoa Bean to Chocolate* (2003).

To determine whether the text she has tentatively selected is appropriately challenging, she searches the Lexile.com website for the title, *From Cocoa Bean to Chocolate*, to determine this book's quantitative level of text difficulty. She finds that this book has a Lexile level of 330, at the upper end of the end-of-year Lexile level stretch bandwidth of 450.

Next, she reads the text carefully and closely to identify potential qualitative comprehension supports or obstacles to be faced by her 1st-grade students when they read this text. The supports/obstacles she notes in this book include: use of a glossary to locate meanings for bolded words, full-color photographs without captions, infrequent use of signal words to cue connections among ideas or text structure, inclusion of very few text features (bolded headings and words), and no numbering of steps in a sequence diagram or illustrations that show the entire process of getting from a cocoa bean to eating chocolate.

Constructing Microstructure to Form a Textbase

After selecting the *From Cocoa Bean to Chocolate* text as appropriately challenging, she carefully reads this informational text again to plan her selection of multiple CCSS Reading Anchor Standards and multiple sets of comprehension strategies to be taught at multiple levels of text comprehension processing. During the first reading of the informational text, Ms. Chang wants to help her students construct a microstructure of the text as represented in the CI text comprehension model. To accomplish this aim, she starts her instruction with CCSS Reading Anchor Standard cluster 1—key ideas and details—and then selects individual Reading Anchor Standard 2, requiring her students *to identify the main topic and be able to retell key details from the text.*

Thus, to support her teaching of CCSS individual Reading Anchor Standard 2, Ms. Chang selects an evidence-based set of two comprehension strategies, paraphrasing and retelling, appropriate for teaching this initial level of text comprehension processing—microstructure construction. Before she begins teaching the text, she reminds her students to activate their background knowledge about chocolate, including what they learned from reading *Curious George Goes to the Chocolate Factory.*

Ms. Chang begins her instruction by reading aloud the first 2 pages of the text. As she reads aloud, she thinks aloud about how she identifies the key idea. As she thinks aloud, she notes that each of the three sentences read aloud on the first two pages of the text is telling about a process. She reads and thinks about the question, what is it that each of the three sentences is telling her about: (1) how farmers plant cocoa bean plants, (2) pods grow on the plants, and (3) seeds grow in the pods. She says to her students, "It seems to me like all of these sentences are telling me about how cocoa beans grow," as is found in the bolded heading. She then thinks aloud and tells her students that thinking about what all of the sentences tell about is one way to identify the key idea in a text. Another is to note that the author has helped the reader by providing a bolded heading in which the key idea is identified. After reading these first 2 pages of the book aloud, Ms. Chang demonstrates how to paraphrase each sentence on the page and how to retell what she has learned from the text so far. The process of modeling identification of the key idea and retelling the key ideas and details in the text by using her own words, or paraphrasing, is guided and gradually released to the students in the subsequent pages while reading the text.

Constructing Macrostructure to Form a Textbase

In the next part of the lesson, Ms. Chang focuses her instruction on helping her students construct a macrostructure of the text, as indicated in the second level of the CI text comprehension model, by selecting individual Reading Anchor Standard 5: Know and use various text features to locate various facts—from within cluster 2—craft and structure. To support teaching of Reading Anchor Standard 5, Ms. Chang selects another evidence-based set of two comprehension strategies appropriate for supporting this higher level of text processing: (1) noting text features (bolded typography and headings), and (2) using a glossary to be used during a second close reading.

She begins this part of the lesson by pointing out bolded words in the text using a computer projector and a document camera so that her students are looking at what she is reading and she can point to "bolded text" items. She points out that the author has provided in the text several bolded headings and some bolded words. She tells her students that authors often use bolded headings to tell the key idea for paragraphs or sections of text to help readers use the key idea(s) to connect to subsequent details to be read in the text. She reads the sentences that follow the bolded heading. She points out through her thinking aloud that individual sentences contain details about the key idea signaled by the author through the use of bolded headings. She reads several more pages in the text and asks students to paraphrase what the sentences following the bolded headings tell about the key idea.

Next, Ms. Chang notes that there are other bolded words within the sentences of the text. She models her thinking that when she sees a bolded word in an informational text, she knows that the author has provided something called a glossary in the back of the book so readers can learn the meaning of the bolded words in the text. As the students and Ms. Change close read the text together, she gradually releases the task of noting bolded words in the sentences of the text and finding their meanings in the book's glossary.

Integration to Form a Situation Model

In the last segment of this CI Model comprehension lesson, Ms. Chang focuses her comprehension instruction on helping her 1st-grade students integrate the textbase information they have constructed in the two previous levels of comprehension instruction with their background knowledge to create a situation model of the text. To do this, she selects individual Reading Anchor Standard 7: Use illustrations and details in a text to describe its key ideas, from within cluster 3—integration of knowledge and ideas. To support her teaching of Reading Anchor Standard 7, Ms. Chang selects yet another evidence-based set of two comprehension strategies appropriate for this next level of text processing: (1) examining illustrations, and (2) describing how illustrations support the text during a third close reading.

Ms. Chang begins this last segment of the lesson by reading aloud details from the text, thinking aloud, and modeling how to annotate text details (see Figure 1.8) for her students. Next she relates how the details she has located and annotated combined with illustrations in the text helped her to make sense of the text. She models how when she reads a detail from the text, *hard pods grow on each tree*, she uses the photograph of a cocoa tree showing many big brown pods to help her to create a visual image in her mind and an understanding of what a pod of cocoa beans looks like. As they close read the text together, Ms. Chang gradually releases responsibility to her students for describing how illustrations help them to understand text details.

Integrating the Situation Model into Background Knowledge

To wrap up the lesson, Ms. Chang selects any other Reading Anchor Standard she feels will help her students solidify their integration of text

Figure 1.8. Annotations Checklist

Student _____ Teacher _____ Date _____

_____ Includes targeted annotation symbols/marks

   [___] Writes numbers to track the sequence of ideas/events

   [___] Circles keywords/phrases that are confusing

   [___] Attempts to use context clues and/or word parts for resolving confusing
        words or phrases

   [___] Underlines the cental idea or major points

   [___] Places symbols in the margin to note key ideas, questions, or summaries

   [___] Writes page numbers to show where related ideas can be found

_____ Includes margin notes that explain the meaning of the symbols/marks

_____ Includes margin notes that indicate use of comprehension strategies

_____ Includes margin notes that reveal personal comments/questions

_____ Includes revised or new annotations based on rereading and/
        or collaborative conversations

_____ Annotations are legible and useful for future oral or written tasks

Comments:

Note. From Fisher, D., & Frey, N. (2015). Contingency teaching during close reading. *The Reading Teacher, 66*(4), 277–286.

information and background knowledge to form a situation model of the text and integrate the situation model into their world knowledge network. She selects individual Reading Anchor Standard 3: Describe connections between two individuals, events, ideas or pieces of information in a text. To meet this standard, Ms. Chang models how to, and asks her students to help her, insert numerical, ordinal, and signal connector words into the text to highlight the sequential process of making chocolate from cocoa beans. Once these words have been inserted, Ms. Chang asks her students to help her create a graphic organizer illustrating the sequential process described in this informational text—the sequence of events that occur in making a cocoa bean into chocolate! This process helps students take the situation model of this text and actively organize the process or sequence and integrate it into their world knowledge networks, described as the final step in the CI Model of Text Comprehension (Kintsch, 2013). Through this carefully planned multilevel comprehension instruction process, Ms. Chang's students have a stronger sense of sequential texts that they can employ in other readings and in their writing of comparable genres. When teachers help their students to read a text using the multileveled processes represented in the CI text comprehension model, students will develop over time into much better readers in general and highly proficient comprehenders of text specifically.

The remainder of this book is intended to help primary-grade classroom (K–2) teachers put their theoretical knowledge of the CI Model of Text Comprehension into practice. Subsequent chapters illustrate how to use the CI Model to plan effective CCSS Reading Standards-based comprehension instruction for young readers, including those who struggle. Extended examples will be provided, using both literature and informational texts, of how to select CCSS Reading Anchor Standards using a multileveled process guided by the three CCSS Reading Anchor Standard categories/clusters, coupled with guidance about how to select and teach sets of evidence-based comprehension strategies at the multiple levels of text processing described in the CI Model. In the final chapter, we describe how teachers can design and use formative assessments to evaluate their students' levels of text comprehension processing and their mastery of the CCSS Reading Anchor Standards and the multiple levels of the CI Model's comprehension text processing. We also will describe how to use assessment data to adapt and modify comprehension lessons to provide extended support for students who struggle with the demands of comprehending increasingly complex texts.

CHAPTER 2

Building Oral Language to Support Reading Comprehension

CHAPTER OVERVIEW

The previous chapter focused on describing Kintsch's (2013) construction–integration processes through which readers comprehend text. This chapter will address how to create a classroom environment that supports oral language acquisition, offer suggestions about how teachers might build oral language that supports the "construction–integration" text comprehension process, and discuss ways in which teachers might leverage the power of oral language across the early grades to build a scaffold for supporting future reading comprehension.

Strong Oral Language Leads to Good Reading Comprehension

Oral language development provides the foundation for learning, reading, and academic success in early childhood because it involves the ability to acquire, practice, and integrate knowledge across the domains of phonology (sound units), semantics (vocabulary), morphology (grammatical morphemes), syntax (grammar), and pragmatics (social use) (Dickinson & Tabors, 2001; Snow, 1993; Tabors & Snow, 2001; Whitehurst & Lonigan, 2001).

Oral language skills such as inferencing and comprehension monitoring at age 7 have been shown to be reliable predictors of later reading comprehension at age 11 (Oakhill & Cain, 2012). In addition, cognitive profiles of elementary school-aged students with reading comprehension difficulties have shown that those students often evidence simultaneous weakness in oral language comprehension and processing (Duff & Clarke, 2011; Duke, Cartwright, & Hilden, 2014). In fact, Catts, Fey, Zhang, and Tomblin (1999) found that approximately 70% of students with poor reading comprehension in 2nd grade also demonstrated significant oral language deficits in kindergarten. Similarly, young students with poor language skills in kindergarten have been shown to be at a higher risk for developing reading comprehension problems in later years (Catts et al., 2002). Importantly, Nation et al. (2010) found that oral language weaknesses in poor comprehenders at age 8 were not a simple consequence of their reading comprehension impairment, but rather reflected persistent prior weaknesses in expressive and receptive language, listening comprehension, and grammatical understanding. As a consequence, weakness in oral language in the early grades is increasingly viewed as a contributing and causal factor affecting poor reading comprehension in later grades (Duke et al., 2014; National Early Literacy Panel [NELP], 2008).

Research shows that oral language accounts for unique variance in later reading comprehension (Cain, Oakhill, & Lemmon, 2004; Casteel & Simpson, 1991; Hogan, Bridges, Justice, & Cain, 2011). For example, Cain et al. (2004) investigated whether higher level oral language skills such as inferencing and comprehension monitoring played unique roles in determining comprehension levels for 100 average readers between the ages of 7 and 8. Findings suggested that these component skills accounted for significant variance in reading comprehension beyond that explained by vocabulary, verbal ability, word reading, and working memory.

Teaching Oral Language Promotes Reading Comprehension

Children learn to integrate knowledge across linguistic domains in speaking contexts that require textual discourse. An emerging body of evidence strongly suggests that early training in higher level oral language skills (e.g., inferencing, comprehension monitoring, complex syntax, and morphology) may result in significant and lasting improvements in later reading comprehension (Clarke, Snowling, Truelove, & Hulme, 2010; Paquette, Fello, & Jalongo, 2007). The strongest evidence to date showing that oral language instruction improves listening and reading comprehension has come primarily from work with narrative texts (Duff & Clarke, 2011; Gillam & Gillam, 2014; Gillam, Gillam, & Reece, 2012; Gillam, Hartzheim, Simonsmeier, & Gillam 2014). However, recent research is replete with reports that students' ability to paraphrase and summarize—two very complex oral language tasks—has been shown to improve comprehension of informational texts (Gajria & Salvia, 1992; Watson, Gable, Gear, & Hughes, 2012; Westby, Culatta, Lawrence, & Hall-Kenyon, 2010).

Strategies taught to improve paraphrasing and summarization typically address the content and organization of summaries but rarely focus on the higher level language abilities that are needed for younger students to be consistently successful in either task. For example, the National Institute for Literacy (2007) proposed a four-step process for students to create a summary: (1) identify and formulate the main ideas, (2) connect the main ideas, (3) identify and delete redundancies, and (4) restate the main ideas and connections using one's own words. The language skills necessary for this level of successful summarization go well beyond teaching vocabulary and basic grammatical knowledge (e.g., past tense). They extend to an understanding of literate language to include cohesion terms (e.g., subordinating and coordinating conjunctions, causal adverbs), complex syntax (e.g., subject and object relative clauses), complex morphology (e.g., derivational, lexical), and specific vocabulary (e.g., Tier 3, signal words). All of these factors contribute to a reader's ability to construct an accurate and complete textbase in service of a coherent situation model to aid in the comprehension and composition of narrative or informational text.

Teaching Higher Level Oral Language Skills in Service of Reading Comprehension

Effective instruction for improving higher level oral language skills targets knowledge of complex syntax, morphological forms (Scott & Nelson, 2009), Tier 2 or 3 vocabulary relevant to narrative and informational texts, and inferencing skills. Efficacious higher level oral language instruction includes the following active ingredients:

1. Explicit instruction in complex syntax (e.g., relative clause) as in, *She ate the pie that was on the counter*; and complex morphology (e.g., derivational suffixes), as in adding the suffix *-able* to the word *read* to form the word *readable*
2. Instruction for content and vocabulary words relevant to student generation of inferences
3. The use of language facilitation devices like focused stimulation (e.g., repeated modeling of copula "are") to provide linguistic input to help students express ideas
4. Answering questions after oral presentation of text

Successful oral language instruction will incorporate training to improve text-based recall of key ideas and specific details from passages, identification of text structures, and the ability to integrate this information (text-based and background knowledge–based) for use in recalling, paraphrasing, retelling, summarizing, and composing in the narrative and informational genres. In other words, students are helped to develop a situation model integrated into each reader's world knowledge network.

SETTING THE STAGE FOR ORAL LANGUAGE INSTRUCTION TO SUPPORT COMPREHENSION

The Common Core State Standards for speaking and listening (CCSS. ELA/Literacy) define the oral language skills and knowledge that students must demonstrate at each grade level if they are to be college and career ready upon exiting school. These include three standards under comprehension and collaboration and three under presentation of knowledge and ideas for each grade level. In kindergarten:

- The first standard under comprehension and collaboration states that students must be able to prepare for and participate in conversations and collaborations with diverse partners, and be able to build on and express ideas with clarity.
- The second standard suggests that students must be able to integrate and evaluate information presented in diverse formats (media, visual, quantitatively, orally).
- The third outlines the importance of the ability to evaluate one's point of view, and use reasoning and evidence during persuasive rhetoric.
- The first skill listed under presentation of knowledge and ideas highlights the importance of a student's ability to present information, findings, and evidence in logical, organized ways that are appropriate to the audience and purpose of the task.
- The last two standards under this heading are the ability to make good use of media and visual displays to express information and enhance understanding, and to adapt speech to be appropriate to different contexts and tasks, with good command of English grammar.

In 1st grade, comprehension and collaboration standards include the ability to:

- Follow agreed-upon rules during discussions
- Build upon others' discussions by commenting and turn-taking
- Ask questions when necessary to improve comprehension

Presentation of knowledge and ideas standards include the ability to describe objects, places, and people with sufficient detail, using drawings to clarify thoughts and feelings, and to produce complete, grammatical sentences when appropriate.

Finally, comprehension and collaboration and presentation of knowledge and ideas standards for 2nd grade are very similar to those outlined for 1st grade; however, they:

- Include more sophisticated topics (grade 2 topics and texts)
- Require that children begin to understand and compose detailed recounts, narratives, and poems

In order to design lessons that allow students opportunities to practice and develop these skills, we must understand the "component" skills that underlie them. What skills enable a student to "prepare for and participate in conversations and collaborations with diverse partners," and "to be able to build on and express ideas with clarity"? Further, what does a student need to know to be able to "describe objects, places, and people with sufficient detail," or to recount stories, or to identify main ideas or to elaborate?

Many if not all of the CCSS go well beyond constructing a textbase and require integration, described in the CI Model as the ability to assimilate information from the textbase (or oral discourse) with the contents of the student's background knowledge to create a situation model. There are basic building blocks that must be in place if students are to be able to accomplish these standards.

The Role of Morphology and Syntax in Constructing a Textbase

The extent of our mental lexicon or library of words increases profoundly over our lifetime as new experiences lead to the development of new knowledge about people, places, things, concepts, ideas, and the words we use to encode them. As children develop more complex thoughts and concepts, they learn new words to express them, and they come up with more and more sophisticated things to say. The expression of complex concepts requires the ability to sequence words together into lengthier and more complex sentences, and eventually discourse. The production of discourse requires the integration of numerous linguistic structures, including those associated with the domains of morphology and syntax.

It is important to note that words do not carry all of the meaning in sentences. Meaning also is expressed through the relationships that words in sentences form when used "together." For example, the word /girl/ has a meaning in and of itself; however, the word /at/ does not. Rather, /at/ indicates a relationship between two meaningful expressions (The girl is at the door).

This example illustrates the fact that some morphemes, such as "girl," which is a lexical morpheme, carry meaning in and of themselves, while others, for example, "at," do not.

All languages have rules for the ways sentences may be constructed, which is referred to as syntax. Knowledge of syntax is important because similar words mean different things when their order is changed. For example, if I said, "*Sally hit John*," we would agree that Sally was the hitter and John was the person who was hit. That isn't the same thing as "*John hit Sally*," even though the actual words in the sentence stayed the same. Our understanding of the word-order constraints of our language, for example, "subject–verb–object," helps us indicate "who did what to whom." Successful communication requires that both speakers and listeners concur on word meanings as well as meaning that is conveyed by word order.

Unfortunately, the capacity to construct grammatical sentences involves more than simple knowledge of word order. In come cases, words must be changed depending on what their role is in the sentence. Patterns that are related to internal word structure are called *morphology*. A morpheme is the smallest grammatical unit that holds meaning. For example, the word *boy* is a morpheme because it cannot be divided further and still hold meaning (neither "b" nor "oy" has any meaning). *Boy* is a *free* morpheme because it can stand alone as a word. However, the plural marker letter "s," pronounced as –z, is a *bound* morpheme. The plural –z is bound because it cannot stand alone and still contain meaning. The plural –z is a grammatical tag or marker in English that, when added to the word *boy*, indicates that there is more than one (boys). The morpheme is grammatical because in English the sentence, *The boys were running*, would be ungrammatical without the –z on the word boy (The boy are running). Other grammatical morphemes include inflections such as the progressive tense marker *–ing* and the past tense marker *–ed*. Most bound morphemes in the English language are *suffixes* that are located at the ends of words.

There are also *derivational* morphemes, such as un– (e.g., *unable*). Derivational morphemes are found at the beginning of words and are referred to as *prefixes*. *Suffixes* are also derivational morphemes and are found at the ends of words, such as the –ly in absolutely. This derivational morpheme changes an adjective (That is the *absolute* solution) to an adverb (I was *absolutely* sure that was the right solution). Understanding derivational morphology requires complex knowledge of lexical, phonological, and syntactic aspects of language, which is why they are not fully acquired well into the school-age years and play a substantial role in academic success (Jarmulowicz & Hay, 2009; Jarmulowicz, Taran, & Hay, 2007).

Interestingly, grammar (form) is somewhat independent of meaning (content). That is, even if speakers use word order incorrectly, it is still possible to understand what they meant to say. For example, a sentence such as, "*Him petted little piggy,*" is not grammatical because an object pronoun (Him) is used in place of the subject; the regular past tense marker is applied to the word *pet*, which should be produced using the form pet; and the child omitted an article *the* or *a* before the object noun phrase little piggy. Even though the sentence is clearly ungrammatical, we are able to determine that the child is describing a male petting a small pig. How is this possible? It is likely that we are able to integrate information into our own world knowledge and construct a situation model even when microstructure is not complete or even coherent. This "top-down" process may be an important part of how we comprehend spoken and written language.

Developing Syntax Sense: Combining Phrases and Clauses to Construct a Textbase

As children mature, they begin to sequence more and more words together using complex phrases, clauses, and sentences. In addition, we begin to notice noun and verb phrase development that involves discrete rules related to word order and syntactic marking that become more complex over time. To illustrate, more complex noun phrases include constituents such as initiators (a few, almost), determiners (articles, quantifiers, demonstratives, possessives), adjectives (ordinals, attributes, possessive nouns), nouns (object and reflexive pronouns, subject, nouns), and modifiers (prepositional phrases, adverbs, embedded clauses, adjectivals).

Similarly, increased use of transitive verbs, in which the verb takes a direct object as in, "*He hit the ball*"; intransitive verbs that do not take the passive form or direct objects like, "*He ran*"; and stative verbs, or verbs that are followed by a complement like, "*I said, come over here,*" results in more complex verb phrases and sentences over time. Verb phrases may include elements such as modal auxiliaries to provide additional information about the function of the main verb that follows it (*may* walk, *shall* walk, *would* walk), perfective auxiliaries that express an action that occurred in the past but remains relevant (They have ridden bikes, She has broken her arm, We had written a play), *be* verbs (are, is, am), negatives (not), passives (been), main verbs (walk, look, ride), prepositional phrases (on the beach), noun phrases (a skunk), noun complements (I saw a teacher), as well as adverbial phrases (run quickly). When these complex microstructure forms are embedded in ongoing discourse, it can make it more difficult for students to identify text macrostructure and to form a coherent situation model of the information for use in future encounters with similar text. Therefore, teachers may want to check for comprehension when more complex discourse is used during instruction. If students demonstrate difficulty when faced with complex language, simpler language may be used, or the teacher may implement instruction in the complex forms.

How do children progress from elaborating on noun and verb phrases to producing complex sentences and finally to understanding and generating discourse? Generally speaking, this is accomplished through a process of phrasal and clausal conjoining and embedding. Phrases and clauses are different in that phrases are utterances that do *not* contain *both* a subject and a verb. So, a phrase has to be embedded in a sentence in order to be grammatical. To illustrate, the phrase, *with my grandmother*, cannot stand alone. To be grammatical, it has to be combined with a subject and a verb such as, *I made a cake with my grandmother.* On the contrary, clauses are grammatical because they contain subjects (nouns) and predicates (verbs), such as *They swam.*

Sentences may contain many clauses. Some sentences contain two main clauses that are joined with a coordinating conjunction (for, and, nor, but, or, yet, so) or may contain subordinated clauses (joined with a word like *because* or *who*). For example, to form a compound sentence using a coordinated clause, you might say, "Casey was painting and she lost her brush." To form a sentence using a subordinated clause, you might say, "The boy who had big eyebrows pushed the child on the teeter totter." In this case, the main clause is, *The boy pushed the child on the teeter totter*. The clause, *The boy had big eyebrows*, is embedded into the main clause to make it clear who the subject was. In general, children conjoin two main clauses and then learn to compose more complex sentences that involve this kind of embedding.

As children are learning to use complex sentences, they also are learning to create complex questions that contain multiple clauses and phrases. For example, yes–no questions that require children to invert auxiliaries, such as in the sentence, "Are you walking to the store?" begin to emerge, as do "tag" questions like, "Let's jump in the mud, okay?" and more complex syntactic utterances such as, "He is really tough, isn't he?"

As children progress into the school-age years, they are required to use more complex language to talk about what they know, and as they do so, they acquire what are called "literate language structures." While oral language is used in daily communication and incorporates nonverbal cues as well as verbal ones (He is handsome), literate language might be used to convey a similar yet more "scholarly" message, such as, "His handsomeness is outshined only by his wisdom." Children with command of literate language have been shown to academically outperform those without it.

There are four broad categories of words that make up literate language: conjunctions, elaborated noun phrases, metacognitive and metalinguistic verbs, and adverbs (Greenhalgh & Strong, 2001). Conjunctions are used to describe the relationship between actions, events, and objects. Three categories of conjunctions that often are taught to improve the use of literate language include temporal conjunctions (e.g., when, while, after), causal conjunctions (e.g., because, so that), and coordinating conjunctions (so, but, however). Temporal conjunctions are used to provide a background for the things that happen in stories. For example, "*When* Sally climbed up the ladder, she looked over the rung to say good night to the spider, Charlotte." On the contrary, causal conjunctions are used to give the reader a physical or psychological reason for the actions that are taking place in the story or event, as in, "The kittens were happy *because* the milk spilled on the floor." Coordinating conjunctions may be used to demonstrate opposition, as in the example, "He swam fast *but* he didn't catch the boat."

Elaborated noun phrases (ENPs) are words or series of words that may be used to enhance descriptions of objects or elements contained in events or stories. Children may elaborate by using noun modifiers (e.g., *the tall, pretty tree*), qualifiers (e.g., the dog walked over the *hill next to the junkyard*), relative clauses (e.g., the lady took home the puppy *that licked her*), and appositives (e.g., this girl, *Joan*, had a pig) (Eisenberg et al., 2008). Metacognitive verbs are used to illustrate what characters might be thinking (e.g., they *thought* they were at the wrong place), and met-alinguistic verbs are used to characterize how speech/language is used in stories (e.g., Mary *yelled*, "Stop!"). Adverbs are mastered well before children enter school and are used to indicate time, manner, or degree, as in the example, "The jeep stopped *quickly* at the ledge of the cliff."

As children enter school, they listen to and read stories, and learn to read and compose their own stories. As they do so, they are exposed to and learn to use a wide variety of complex sentences and discourse structures. Continued experience with written language, which contains more complex sentences than oral conversational language, is strongly associated with gains in the understanding and use of complex language for navigating narrative (stories) and expository (informational) texts.

There are significant memory demands that are necessary for children to be able to conjoin and embed phrases and clauses into complex sentences. That is, children must be able to hold information in their mind as they listen to and integrate new information into their memory. Working memory is a series of mental processes that are used to hold information in the center of attention so it may be used to complete cognitive tasks (Baddeley & Hitch, 2000). Learning language relies on working memory specifically as it relates to focusing one's attention on the spoken or written word, associating words with their literal or relational meanings within sentences, and relating the meanings to some experience, concept, or knowledge base that is stored in long-term memory (Gillam, Montgomery, & Gillam, 2009). If a sentence contains a syntactic structure (e.g., a passive sentence such as, As she wandered down the street, she thought about what she might do for dinner) that is new or unfamiliar, it must be remembered using (1) the word sequence, (2) the bound grammatical morphemes attached to the free morphemes, (3) the context in which the sentence was spoken, and (4) the role the words had in the utterance (subject, verb, object, modifier, etc.).

Most children are capable of managing, processing, and storing complex linguistic information so they can remember it and figure out what a new syntactic structure might mean. As children encounter a language structure multiple times, they begin to recognize it, and thus discover how old and new words, phrases, clauses, and structures may be combined to form novel sequences (Maratsos, 1990; Mintz, Newport, & Bever, 2002; Redington, Chater, & Finch, 1998; Tomasello, 2003). We can capitalize on students' natural "pattern-finding abilities" in the classroom to facilitate the use of higher level syntactic structures in service of reading comprehension.

HOW DO WE FACILITATE USE OF HIGHER LEVEL SYNTACTIC STRUCTURES?

Research has shown that using language facilitation techniques like focused stimulation, recasting, vertical structuring, prompts, and questions 70–75% of the time during conversations with students improves students' use of various syntactic forms. We also can facilitate the use of "text patterns" such as problem–solution or cause–effect. Facilitation techniques include *focused stimulation, expansions, vertical structures, prompts,* and *questions.*

Focused stimulation is when the teacher demonstrates the use of a syntactic form or text pattern in a functional context and gives students an opportunity to use it. However, they are not required to do so. These demonstrations are repeated in contrastive sentences, as in the following example using the auxiliary *is*, "She is walking home. Wait, is she walking home? I think she is!" Focused stimulation also may be used to demonstrate a text pattern, as in the following example of a cause–effect structure. In the book *Beyond 'Oh'ia Valley: Adventures in a Hawaiian Rainforest* (Matsumoto, 1996), a young tree snail learns about the impact of invasive species on the land, animals, and ecosystem in a Hawaiian rainforest. To illustrate cause–effect, the teacher might read from the portion of the book that describes how the rainforest was so beautiful until the pigs destroyed the ferns, and that they did not belong in the valley. Then, the teacher might emphasize the causal connective word "because," saying that "because the pigs came to the valley (cause) the ferns were destroyed (effect). . . ." The teacher would continue to use this kind of focused stimulation to highlight the many cause–effect relationships in the book. By highlighting the text structure, the teacher is supporting the development of a macrostructure and eventually the development of a situation model that may be used for future encounters with similar information.

Similarly, recasting is a technique in which a teacher provides a contingent verbal response to increase the length or complexity of the child's utterance so that a new form is likely to be used. For example, the student might say, "That's a dog," to which the teacher might say, "Is that a dog? I think it is a beautiful dog. What do you think about the dog?" The utterances the teacher used were "contingent" because they incorporated aspects of the child's utterance (talking about a dog), and they were an expansion because they also provided the student with examples of a linguistic input pattern using the auxiliary *is* form being targeted during the interaction.

Consider the following interaction surrounding a discussion of the book *Beyond the 'Ohi'a Valley*. The student might say, "The pigs destroyed the ferns," to which the teacher might say, "You are right. Because the pigs came, the ferns are destroyed." This response is contingent because it incorporated aspects of the student's utterance, and it also highlighted the hierarchical structure of the text (cause–effect). By highlighting the structure, the teacher may assist the student in using it to create a situation model of the text.

A somewhat more sophisticated language facilitation device is called vertical structuring. In vertical structuring, the teacher asks the child a question that will elicit one clause, then another. When both clauses have been elicited, the teacher will "connect" the clauses to construct a complex sentence. For example, the teacher may point to a picture of a child crying and say, "This child is crying. How do you think he feels?" The child may answer, "Sad," after which the teacher asks, "Why do you think he's sad?" The child may then say, "Because his toy is broken." The teacher may then put the two clauses together to say, "The boy is sad because his toy is broken." In this way, the teacher can model the more complex sentence, using the utterances elicited during discussions with the child. Imagine the teacher is using a vertical-structuring technique to facilitate the use of auxiliary inversion questions. The teacher may go one more step in the previous example and add, "Is the child crying because he is sad? Yes, he is crying because he is sad." In this fashion, the pattern of using the auxiliary *is* as an inverted question is illustrated repetitively, giving the student multiple opportunities to hear it and remember it for future use.

To highlight a text structure, the teacher might say, "How were the ferns in the valley destroyed?" to which the student might say, "The pigs destroyed the ferns." The teacher might then ask, "Why were the ferns destroyed?" The student might then say, "Because the pigs came into the valley when they didn't belong there." The teacher would combine the utterances produced by the student to highlight the hierarchical structure, saying, "Yes, the ferns were destroyed because the pigs came into the valley when they didn't belong there." Again, the language facilitation device is used to highlight the text structure (cause–effect) in order to facilitate the development of a situation model of information contained in the book.

One last language facilitation device is the use of prompts and questions. Prompts and questions are used to extend what the student has said or written. For example, the child might say, "The ant is hiding under the mushroom," and the teacher might say, "Who is hiding under the mushroom? I think it's an insect." The question and prompt make it possible for the child to locate the referent (ant) and answer the question accurately. To highlight text structure, the teacher might simply say, "What caused the ferns to be destroyed?" to which the student might say, "The pigs came to the valley when they didn't belong there." The teacher might ask, "What was the effect of the pigs coming to the valley?" The student would answer, "They destroyed all the ferns." This more explicit language facilitation device also may be useful for highlighting various text structure patterns for use in the construction–integration process.

Additional examples of the use of language facilitation devices for eliciting different kinds of syntactic structures and text patterns are provided in Figure 2.1.

ORAL LANGUAGE LESSONS FOR SPEAKING AND LISTENING STANDARDS

As described in Chapter 1, the construction process of the Construction–Integration Model of Text Comprehension involves two levels of text-based comprehension processing: a *microstructure* and a *macrostructure*. The microstructure and macrostructure levels are combined to form the *textbase*, which is a replica of the text (or in the case of oral language, spoken discourse) that is created by the reader or listener. The representation reflects the concepts, ideas, and relationships that are expressed by the words, phrases, clauses, and sentences, and is a reflection of what the text explicitly states. The integration process, on the other hand, involves connecting the information contained in the textbase to the reader's experiences, knowledge, and expectations about the world. It is this process that is used to create a *situation model* or interpretation of what the text means.

This section presents examples of CI theory–grounded oral language lessons for the CCSS Speaking and Listening Standards. The sample lessons illustrated in this chapter have been organized to represent one

Figure 2.1. Use of Language Facilitation Techniques to Encourage Higher Level Language Use

A. Focused stimulation

Definition: Repeated use of a sentence pattern
Examples:
> *Sentence pattern:* Subordinating adverbial clause marking time
>> <u>Before she ate the porridge,</u> Goldilocks made sure nobody was home.
> *Sentence pattern:* Subordinating adverbial clause marking condition
>> You have to sneak up behind the rabbit <u>if you want to catch him.</u>
> *Text pattern:* Cause–effect
>> The Hawaiian rainforest once contained many beautiful ferns until the pigs came and destroyed them. The pigs do not belong in the valley. Because they came, we have no more ferns. The pigs came (cause) and they destroyed all the ferns (effect).

B. Expansions

Definition: Contingent verbal responses that increase the length or complexity of the child's utterance
Examples:
> *Sentence pattern:* Relative causes
>> *Child:* That boy who told was in trouble.
>> *Teacher:* Subjective—Yes, the boy <u>who told on you</u> got in trouble at recess.
>> *Child:* That boy told.
>> *Teacher:* Objective—Yes, I saw the boy <u>who told on you.</u>
> *Text pattern:* Cause–effect
>> *Child:* The pigs destroyed the ferns.
>> *Teacher:* Because the pigs came, the ferns were destroyed.

C. Vertical structuring

Definition: Teacher asks questions to construct a syntactically complete sentence using a complex syntactic form
Examples:
> *Sentence pattern:* Clausal complements
>> *Teacher:* What was the boy doing?
>> *Child:* He was thinking.
>> *Teacher:* What was he thinking?
>> *Child:* That the other kid was mean.
>> *Teacher:* He <u>thought</u> the other kid was mean.
> *Sentence pattern:* Subordinated adverbial clause (showing causal relationships)
>> *Teacher:* What did the character say?
>> *Child:* That he wanted to get under the mushroom.
>> *Teacher:* Why did he want to get under the mushroom?
>> *Child:* Because it was raining and he was getting wet.
>> *Teacher:* He wanted to get under the mushroom <u>because</u> he was getting wet.
> *Text pattern:* Problem–solution
>> *Teacher:* What was happening to the people in William's village?

Figure 2.1, *continued*

> *Student:* They were having trouble surviving.
> *Teacher:* That's a problem.
> *Teacher:* What did William do to help his people?
> *Student:* He built a windmill to make electricity.
> *Teacher:* That was his solution. The people in William's village were having trouble surviving, so he built a windmill to make electricity.

D.   Prompts and questions

Definition: Comments and questions that serve to extend what the student has said or written
Examples:
> *Sentence pattern:* Infinitives
> > *Child:* Goldilocks wanted the porridge.
> > *Teacher:* Why did she want the porridge?
> > *Child:* To eat it.
> > *Teacher:* Yes, Goldilocks wanted <u>to eat</u> the porridge.
> *Text pattern:* Problem–solution
> > *Teacher:* Why did William build a windmill?
> > *Student:* To make electricity.
> > *Teacher:* Why did William want to make electricity?
> > *Student:* To help his people survive.
> > *Teacher:* William's village was having trouble surviving (problem) so he built a windmill to make electricity (solution).

Note: When children make grammatical errors, teachers' recasting should model the correct usage. Teachers may choose to ask the child to repeat the sentence correctly, but this imitation practice is not necessary.
Example:
> *Child:* Them walked home.
> *Teacher:* Yes, they walked home.

Example:
> *Child:* How they did that?
> *Teacher:* How did they do that?

---

section of the three comprehension levels (microstructure, macrostructure, situation model) using CCSS Speaking and Listening Standards for each of the primary (K–2) grade levels.

The sample lesson provided here is designed for kindergarten students; however, it may be easily adapted for use with older students. The lessons present examples of how to teach through each level of the CI Model—constructing a microstructure of the text, constructing a macrostructure of the text, and integration to create a situation model—while focusing on teaching auxiliary inversion questions, a complex language function needed for understanding text.

STRENGTHENING ORAL LANGUAGE SKILLS:
A FOCUS ON THE MICROSTRUCTURE
IN THE KINDERGARTEN CLASSROOM

Step 1. Standard 2: Comprehension and Collaboration

In kindergarten, the second standard under comprehension and collaboration states that students must be able to confirm understanding of a text read aloud or information presented orally (or through other media) by asking and answering questions about key details and requesting clarification if something is not understood. Our kindergarten teacher, Miss Barnes, knows that linguistic input has a strong effect on how children learn new syntactic forms (Finneran & Leonard, 2011). Therefore, she is going to employ some evidence-based language facilitation strategies for promoting the use of "auxiliary inversion question forms" during discussions surrounding children's literature books.

Miss Barnes has selected *Mushroom in the Rain* (Ginsburg, 1974), a story that contains a repetitive but variable episode structure, to target children's use of auxiliary inversions (e.g., Can he hide under the mushroom? Is he hiding under the mushroom? Yes, he is!). This book is appropriate for guided reading at the kindergarten level and is available as an audio book. Since the focus of this lesson is to heighten oral language, children will listen to the book on audio as Miss Barnes flips through the pages, and later they will act it out. Miss Barnes knows that this book may be used to foster auxiliary question forms through repetitive episodes and then a slight variation in the episode that has been shown to promote learning of new syntactic forms. The Lexile level of the book is 380L, which is below the grade band for grades 2–3 of 450–725L, so Miss Barnes decides that it is appropriate for use in reading aloud to her kindergarten students.

Miss Barnes reads the book closely to determine potential supports and obstacles in the story. She identifies the following items:

- *Quantitative Supports*—There are many high-frequency words, the sentences are of appropriate length, there are multiple repetitions of the episodes and novel words presented so the new syntactic structure may be encountered often.
- *Qualitative Supports*—The illustrations match the text that is presented; the episode structure is simple and repetitive, with clear identification of the problem faced by the characters.

- *Quantitative Obstacles*—Difficult words include wonder, caught, barely, drenched, huddled, hardly, knew, and know. The words are used in context and are presented in a repeating episode. They will be discussed explicitly during the literature unit so that students will be familiar with their meanings.
- *Qualitative Obstacles*—The illustrations are colorful and engaging, and do not present any notable obstacles.
- *Reader–Task Considerations*—The text fits well with the identified task of fostering the use of different question types and is an engaging story.

Miss Barnes decides to use *Mushroom in the Rain* as one of the texts for promoting students' abilities to ask and answer questions about key details and to request clarification using auxiliary question forms.

Step 2. Constructing a Microstructure of the Text

Miss Barnes selects CCSS.ELA/Literacy.SL.K.2: Confirm understanding of a text read aloud or information presented orally or through other media by asking and answering questions about key details and requesting clarification if something is not understood. Next, she considers the language facilitation strategies that will foster students' ability to ask factual questions about characters and their actions, using auxiliary inversion question forms. She decides to use focused stimulation to highlight the auxiliary inversion question forms used in the book, and to employ recasting to increase the likelihood that the students will use the auxiliary form during discussions. These two procedures were selected because the literature provides considerable support for their success with grammatical targets (Leonard, 1998). Miss Barnes will use a graphic organizer to help students with this task (see Figure 2.2 for graphic organizer). Miss Barnes knows the ability to understand and use auxiliary question forms is an important linguistic skill that students will need to have to be able to participate in literature-based discussions in the classroom. Using explicit instruction, discussion, and role-playing, her lesson (see Figure 2.3 for lesson) will teach students how to ask and answer questions using auxiliary inverted questions to identify the characters and major events in the text.

Figure 2.2. Graphic Organizer Example for Problem Solution

Problem–Solution (PS)	Signal Words and Guiding Questions
Problem ⟶ Solution	Problem, question, issue, trouble, solution, answer, response, puzzle, issue, trouble, response to solve the problem
	Is there a problem?
	What is the problem?
	What should they do to solve the problem?
	What did they do to solve the problem?
	Have you had a similar experience?
	What did you do to solve the problem?

Step 3: Constructing a Macrostructure of the Text

The first sample lesson was designed to practice using auxiliary inversion question forms while constructing a microstructure (CI Model Step 2) of the story *Mushroom in the Rain* (Ginsburg, 1989). To allow students to practice CI Model Step 3, Miss Barnes will prepare and teach additional lessons based on the Construction–Integration Model using *Mushroom in the Rain* and then a new text to build students' comprehension skills.

> **Lesson Objective/Explanation:** (Teacher wording is in italics.) *Today we are going to see if we can "retell the story"* Mushroom in the Rain *without looking at the pages. Let's listen again to the story (play audio book) but this time, I want you to notice that each new paragraph in this story begins with an event that motivates a character into action. Remember, it is raining, and this makes the ant want to get out of the rain. Each animal takes an action because of the rain, or, in the case of the rabbit, being chased by a fox. Then, each animal is able to reach their goal of getting out of the rain. How did they do this? Yes, by hiding under the mushroom. So, do they hide under the mushroom? Yes, they do!* (Teacher will provide focused stimulation for auxiliary inversion questions [is, can, does] throughout the lesson and use contingent recasts when students produce the auxiliary in sentences.)
>
> 1. Teacher plays the audio version of *Mushroom in the Rain*.
> 2. Teacher says, " *Who can remember what animal got wet first? Yes, it was the ant. What was our question about the ant? Yes, can he get under the mushroom? Well, did he get under the mushroom? Yes, he did get under the mushroom. How did he do that? Yes, as it rained, the*

Figure 2.3. Lesson 1: Teaching Auxiliary Inversion While Supporting Construction of Text Microstructure

CCSS Anchor Standard: Comprehension and Collaboration: CCSS.ELA/Literacy. SL.K.2: Confirm understanding of a text read aloud or information presented orally or through other media by asking and answering questions about key details and requesting clarification if something is not understood.

Materials: An enlarged copy of *Mushroom in the Rain* (Ginsburg, 1989) and the audio version for children to listen to while Miss Barnes shows the pages. Sentence strips with blanks for the auxiliary forms. Costumes, pictures, or masks to represent each of the characters in the book.

Book Overview

Character	Initiating Event	Attempt	Complication	Consequence
Ant	Caught in rain	Where can I hide		Hides under mushroom
Butterfly	So wet, can't fly	Let me come in from the rain	Can't let you in, no room	Made room for butterfly
Mouse	Drenched to the bone	Let me come in under the mush-room	No more room	Huddled closer and let mouse in
Sparrow	Feathers are drip-ping, wings are tired	Let me under mush-room to dry out and rest	No room	Moved over and there was room for the sparrow
Rabbit	Fox chasing me	Hide me		Crowded them-selves and let him in
Fox came	Have you seen rabbit		No way rabbit is here, no room	Fox ran off
	Rain over	Everyone came out from un-der mush-room	Can't believe they all fit	Mushrooms grow when it rains

Figure 2.3. Lesson 1, *continued*

Lesson Objective/Explanation: (Teacher wording is in italics.) *Today we are going to listen to a story about a bunch of animals who need to get out of the rain. The interesting thing is they all hide in a very unlikely place, under a mushroom. The problem in the story is that all of the animals want to get under the mushroom, but they have trouble believing they'll fit. We will ask two questions during the story. The first is, "Can the animal get under the mushroom?" and the other is, "Is the animal under the mushroom?"*

1. Teacher plays the audio version of *Mushroom in the Rain* while showing the pictures to the class.

2. *Did you listen carefully and think about our questions? Can the animal get under the mushroom? Did the animal get under the mushroom? I'm going to read through this story again and you say the word /is/ when it is the right time. I'll show you how to do the first one. I will write your answer into the chart. See the first one? Here is the ant. He's all wet. OK look at the next page. <u>Blank</u> the ant hiding under the mushroom? What goes in the blank? Yes, /is/! Is the ant hiding under the mushroom? That's right. OK, the next part says, The ant <u>blank</u> hiding under the mushroom. What goes in the blank? Yes, /is/. The ant is hiding under the mushroom. Let's say both sentences. Is the ant hiding under the mushroom? Yes, The ant is hiding under the mushroom!* The teacher continues to go through the sentences, showing the pages in the book that go with each one.

Focused stimulation chart for /is/

- __ the ant hiding under the mushroom? The ant __ hiding under the mushroom.
- __ the butterfly going to hide under the mushroom? The butterfly __ going to hide under the mushroom.
- __ the mouse hiding under the mushroom? The mouse __ hiding under the mushroom.
- __ the sparrow going to hide under the mushroom? The sparrow __ going to hide under the mushroom.
- __ the rabbit hiding under the mushroom? The rabbit __ hiding under the mushroom.
- __ the fox going to hide under the mushroom? The fox __ NOT going to hide under the mushroom.
- __ the mushroom bigger after the rain? The mushroom __ bigger after the rain.

3. Teacher passes out the costumes and scripts so students can conduct the "play" of *The Mushroom in the Rain*. The teacher will advance the pages as the students act out the story. Full-class participation should make this a very fun activity. Teacher says, *"OK, now we will use the word /can/ just like we used the word /is/. So, we might ask, "Can the ant get under the mushroom? At first, all the animals think they can't! But in the end, they can!* [Teacher then begins the play.]

Script for /can/ auxiliary inversion questions

Ant—Oh no, it's raining and I'm caught in the rain. Can I get under the mushroom? Class: You can't. There is no room. Ant: Wait. I can get under the mushroom.

Figure 2.3. Lesson 1, *continued*

Butterfly—Oh no, it's raining and I'm so wet I can't fly. Can I get under the mushroom? Class: You can't. There is no room. Butterfly: Wait. I can get under the mushroom.

Mouse—Oh no, it's raining and I'm drenched to the bone. Can I get under the mushroom? Class: You can't. There is no room. Mouse: Wait. I can get under the mushroom.

Sparrow—Oh no, it's raining and my feathers are dripping. Can I get under the mushroom? Class: You can't. There is no room. Sparrow: Wait. I can get under the mushroom.

Rabbit—Oh no, a fox is chasing me. Can I get under the mushroom to hide? Class: Hurry, can you move! Rabbit: Thanks, I can get under the mushroom.

Fox—Hey, have you seen a rabbit? Class: No! You can't. There's no room! (Fox walks away.)

Class—Can a mushroom grow in the rain? Yes, it can!

Lesson Conclusion: Teacher reviews with students the /is/, /can/, and /do/ questions and answers, emphasizing how asking and answering these questions has helped to increase their understanding of the story.

---

mushroom got bigger, so the ant was able to get under the mushroom. Who was the next animal? Teacher continues reading and guides the discussion about the events in the story. The teacher will refer to a graphic organizer that contains icons representing the character, the initiating event (goal that prompts the characters into action), the actions taken by characters, and the consequences (the results of their actions) that are in the story (see Figure 2.3). With this information provided by their teacher, the students may be better able to construct a coherent mental model of *Mushroom in the Rain* at a global level, called a *macrostructure*. When the teacher points out that there are hierarchical relationships among the events in the story that follow a particular organizational pattern or text structure, it makes the information contained in the story more memorable (easily stored in long-term memory) for use with future encounters with similar texts. In the case of the *Mushroom in the Rain*, the text structure is a classic narrative. After readers have constructed a textbase (microstructure and macrostructure), the next level of processing is *integration* or *interpretation* of the information that has been encountered.

Step 4: Building a Situation Model

Lesson Objective: Students will now encounter a new story that is in some ways similar to *Mushroom in the Rain* called *Hiding in Rain*

Forests (Creature Camouflage) by Deborah Underwood (2010). The book introduces readers to rainforest habitats and the animals that live there. The focus of the book is on the camouflage techniques that the animals use to hide in the forest in order to survive. The Lexile level of the book is 640L, which is within the grade band for grades 2–3 of 450-725L. The teacher will read the book *Hiding in Rain Forests* using focused stimulation and recasting, with lessons similar to those employed during activities for *Mushroom in the Rain*.

After the children listen to and discuss the new book, the teacher will ask the same kinds of questions as for *Mushroom in the Rain* (teacher wording is in italics): *Can the frog hide in the forest? Did the animal hide in the forest? How did the frog hide in the forest? I'm going to read through this story again and you say the word /is/ when it is the right time. I'll show you how to do the first one. I will write your answer into the chart. See the first one? Here is the frog. He's trying to hide in the forest. Look at the next page.* Blank *the frog hiding in the tree? What goes in the blank? Yes, /is/! Is the frog hiding in the tree, that's right. OK, the next part says, The lizard* blank *hiding on the log. What goes in the blank? Yes, /is./ The lizard is hiding on the log. Let's say both sentences. Is the lizard hiding on the log? Yes, the lizard is hiding on the log!* The teacher continues to go through the sentences, showing the pages in the book that go with each one.

As the teacher continues through the story using auxiliary inversion question forms, she also will point out that each new paragraph in this story begins with a problem that motivates the character to take action to solve it (solution), just like in the *Mushroom in the Rain* book. Each animal hides in a different way in order to survive. In *Mushroom in the Rain*, each animal hides under the mushroom to stay dry. Cross-textual comparisons related to text structure will be made between the two books to highlight the hierarchical structure of the texts (problem–solution) and to help students draw on their own experiences and world knowledge to create a situation model. For example, the teacher will point out that the rain (problem) prompted the animals to hide under the mushroom (solution), and the need to survive (problem) prompted the animals to hide in various ways in the forest (solution). Then, she will highlight the fact that the animals in both stories take actions that result in their solving a problem (to get out of the rain or to survive). A Venn diagram or other organizing framework may be used to facilitate these comparisons.

Even though the original focus of the lesson is to facilitate the use of auxiliary question forms, it is important to help students recognize the identifiable structure(s) of texts that make the construction of a glob-ally coherent model of the text (macrostructure) more memorable and available for use with future encounters with similar texts. In this way, the use of auxiliary question forms may be more likely to be retrieved for later use.

Step 5: Merging the Situation Model into World Knowledge

The situation model or interpretation of the text(s) must then be stored in long-term memory if it is to be useful in the future. This requires "strategic action and effort" on the part of the student. In the texts, *Mushroom in the Rain* and *Hiding in the Rain Forest,* students form a situation model of the content in the text by integrating it with ideas, or experiences stored in their network of world knowledge about times when they needed to get out of the rain or the cold, or times when people needed help to survive. For example, they may link the contents of the textbase that was constructed to personal experiences with being in the rain or snow—such as being caught in the rain at the bus stop, skiing, or forgetting to put on gloves or a hat before going outside in the cold. When students integrate the ideas represented in the textbase with their network of world and experiential background knowledge, they create a situation model or interpretation of the text.

To complete the integration process, students must assimilate the contents of the situation model held in working memory into their world knowledge network stored in long-term memory. As stated in Chapter 1, students will need assistance if they are to take conscious, active steps to integrate the contents of the situation model into their network of world knowledge. In the next lesson, the teacher will help the students consciously link the concept of "helping others" or "get-ting out of the rain or snow" to experiences they have had to compare and contrast the two books (rain vs. snow) and to list their own experi-ences that may be similar in nature. The teacher also will lead students in discussions about what they might do if someone asked them for help. These examples will be written on the board. Students may then be broken into cooperative groups to develop their own stories based on the experiences listed. Students may take turns telling their stories, summarizing the stories that other groups have created, and recounting the experiences of the animals in *Mushroom in the Rain* and *Hiding in the Rain Forest.*

THE BENEFITS OF USING KINTSCH'S CI MODEL AND CCSS
TO TEACH ORAL LANGUAGE

Research has shown that oral language forms the basis for later text comprehension. There are a number of theoretical explanations why knowledge of higher level oral language abilities and the ability to construct microstructure, macrostructure, and situation model levels of discourse may impact comprehension, summarization, retelling, and composition of narrative and informational discourse. Text-processing theories, such as the Construction–Integration Model discussed throughout this book, suggest that sensitivity to text structure affects the organization of information in working memory (Kintsch, 2004; Kintsch & van Dijk, 1978; Meyer & Wijkumar, 2007). CI theory highlights the importance of creating a template textbase (extracting from text macrostructure and microstructure meaning units/propositions), developing a situation model (integration of propositions/meaning units with the reader's background knowledge), and forming connections between the situation model and background knowledge in long-term memory (using syntax, morphology, and vocabulary knowledge) to fully integrate text-based knowledge into one's world knowledge base.

Kintsch draws a clear distinction between "recalling text" (construction of a textbase) and "learning from text" (integration of the situation model into the reader's world knowledge). Individuals tend to form superordinate "concepts" to which subsequent information is "connected" (Kintsch, 2004). Thus, comprehension, whether oral or written, depends fundamentally on the ability to construct information contained in propositions or meaning units across multiple sentences in the text, hold them in memory, and then answer questions and/or recount the information orally or in written form (Williams et al., 2009). Higher level language skills account for unique variance in reading comprehension above and beyond even these skills and must be considered as instructional targets throughout students' classroom experiences. As you read the next chapter, which presents information about the importance of using literature for comprehension instruction, think about how the kinds of language skills discussed in this chapter support the comprehension of literature and impact the way we think about teaching students to understand what they are reading. The linguistic underpinnings of oral and written discourse include knowledge of phonology (sound units), semantics (vocabulary), morphology (grammatical morphemes), syntax (grammar), and pragmatics (social use). Foundational language skills in each of these domains are necessary for proficient comprehension.

CHAPTER 3

Designing Instruction to Teach Literature Comprehension

CHAPTER OVERVIEW

The previous chapter focused on how teachers can build the oral language foundations necessary to help younger students create coherent cognitive representations of the ideas in the texts read aloud by their teachers. This chapter presents information about the importance of using literature for comprehension instruction, suggests resources for selecting literature, and provides three sample lessons intended to illustrate how to use the Construction–Integration Model of Text Comprehension when teaching CCSS ELA Standards for Reading Literature in primary-grade (K–2) classrooms.

Comprehending Literature

Comprehension instruction should be a prominent focus in the primary-grade classroom. The old adage, "learn to read and then read to learn," puts young children at a disadvantage (Pearson & Duke, 2002; Snow, Burns, & Griffin, 1998). The purpose of reading is to gain knowledge, develop an increased understanding of the world, and (hopefully) enjoy the time spent in doing so. While it is crucial for young children to learn the foundational skills of reading that enable automaticity and confidence in word recognition and decoding, primary-grade instruction also can include the use of literature to expand students' world knowledge. Children who "read with understanding at an early age gain access to a broader range of text, knowledge, and educational opportunities" (Shanahan et al., 2010, p. 5).

Young students have significantly more exposure to literature than to any other type of text (Paris & Paris, 2003; Tompkins, Guo, & Justice, 2013). Thus, the use of literature provides a strong foundation for comprehension instruction in the primary grades (Allington, 2009; Barone, 2015). Teachers can build on students' experiences with familiar favorites and extend their knowledge through exposure to new stories and poems. Through literature, students learn to explore possibilities, gain connectedness, develop creative reasoning, and ponder other perspectives (Langer, 2011). Readers laugh at the unexpected happenings of Amelia Bedelia (Parrish, 1991), cry when Old Dan and Little Ann die (Rawls, 1961), cheer when the mouse gets his motorcycle (Clearly, 1965), and learn about friendship from Charlotte and Wilbur (White, 1952). Without quality literature, meaningful reading instruction cannot happen (Raphael, 2000).

Research has shown that literature supports literacy development in several areas. It increases reading comprehension (Duke et al., 2011); facilitates oral language development (NELP, 2008; Potocki, Ecalle, & Magnan, 2013); allows examination of cultural and historical influences on individuals (Hiebert, 2012); cultivates positive attitudes toward reading (Block & Mangieri, 2002); and develops writing ability (Watanabe & Hall-Kenyon, 2011). Children's literature provides the authentic context in which cognitive, social, and emotional interactions take place (Morrow, Tracey, & Healey, 2013). It for these reasons the Common Core State Standards for ELA and Literacy support the use of literature with young students, moving toward a 50/50 balance in the reading of literature and of informational texts by grade 4 (NGA Center & CCSSO, 2010).

The importance of using literature with primary-grade students continues to be emphasized, with cautions for teachers to be wary of shifting the pendulum too far in one direction in the quest to provide content knowledge (Barone, 2015; Hiebert, 2012). The use of literature may be especially important for young children as comprehension of informational text is highly dependent on the reader's existing world knowledge (McNamara, 2009). Young children, especially those who struggle, may lack the prerequisite knowledge for comprehension of informational text. Fortunately, the use of literature can help to build a storehouse of world knowledge for primary-grade students (Neuman & Roskos, 2012). Teachers have long emphasized the importance of time spent reading for the development of reading skills and for building disciplinary and world knowledge. The CCSS for ELA and Literacy also emphasize the importance of reading a range of texts. Comprehension instruction in the primary grades should expose students to a full range of literature and informational texts.

SETTING THE STAGE FOR COMPREHENSION INSTRUCTION
WITH LITERATURE

The Common Core State Standards for ELA and Literacy (CCSS ELA/ Literacy) define literature for grade K–5 students as stories and poetry (grades 6–12 also include drama). Biographies (autobiographies and similar texts) are classified as a category of informational text called literary nonfiction (NGA Center & CCSSO, 2010). With more than 250,000 new children's books published in the past decade and currently in print, and over 20,000 new books for children published annually in the United States, selection of literature for comprehension instruction may seem a daunting task (*Children's Books in Print*, 2015). Appendix A of the CCSS for ELA/Literacy provides helpful information to aid with text selection. One of the key features of the CCSS is a focus on the complexity of text that children read. Anchor Standard 10 (range of reading and level of text complexity) is dedicated specifically to having students read "high-quality, increasingly challenging" texts. Text complexity can be evaluated by consideration of qualitative, quantitative, and reader–task analyses, as discussed in Chapter 2 and seen in examples in this chapter. Appendix B of the CCSS for ELA/Literacy provides examples of stories and poetry for K–12 deemed to meet the criteria for text complexity, quality, and range.

Criteria for evaluating literature also have been established by several professional organizations that present awards to honor literary merit. These awards also may help teachers locate high-quality literature for use with elementary students. Some of the major children's book awards for literature are listed below.

Caldecott Medal & Honor Awards: www.ala.org/alsc/awardsgrants/bookmedia/ caldecottmedal/caldecottmedal

> Presented annually to the illustrator of the most distinguished picture book published in the United States for excellence of: (a) pictorial interpretation of story, theme, or concept; (b) appropriateness of style of illustration to the story, theme, or concept; and (c) plot, theme, characters, setting, mood, or information through the pictures.

Newbery Medal & Honor Awards: www.ala.org/alsc/awardsgrants/bookmedia/ newberymedal/newberymedal

> Presented annually for the most distinguishable contribution to children's literature published in the United States for excellence of: (a) interpretation of the theme or concept; (b) presentation of information, including accuracy, clarity, and organization; (c) development of plot, characters, and setting; and (d) appropriateness of style.

Coretta Scott King Award: www.ala.org/emiert/cskbookawards

> Presented annually to outstanding African American authors and illustrators of books for children and young adults that demonstrate an appreciation of African American culture and universal human values.

Pura Belprè Award: www.ala.org/alsc/awardsgrants/bookmedia/belpremedal

> Presented annually to a Latino/Latina writer and illustrator whose work best portrays, affirms, and celebrates the Latino cultural experience in an outstanding work of literature for children and youth.

Boston Globe/Horn Book Awards:
> www.hbook.com/boston-globe-horn-book-awards/

> Presented annually for children's literature to recognize high quality and overall creative excellence.

Schneider Family Book Award:
> www.ala.org/awardsgrants/schneider-family-book-award

> Presented annually to an author or illustrator for a book that embodies an artistic expression of the disability experience for child and adolescent audiences.

Other Notable Awards:
- International Literacy Association Children's Book Awards
- NCTE Award for Excellence in Poetry for Children
- New York Times Best Illustrated Children's Books of the Year

Of course, visiting with colleagues about books, reading book reviews, browsing bookstores (online and in person), and engaging in wide reading are also excellent ways to become familiar with a range of high-quality children's literature to use with comprehension instruction. Sharing wonderful new books and old favorites seems to bring joy to readers young and old!

SAMPLE COMPREHENSION LESSONS FOR TEACHING READING STANDARDS FOR LITERATURE

The CCSS ELA/Literacy Anchor Standards present a scaffold of instruction designed to enhance students' comprehension abilities that is well supported by research and seems to naturally align with Kintsch's Construction–Integration Model of Text Comprehension (Duke et al., 2011). As discussed in Chapter 1, Reading Anchor Standards 1–3 (cluster 1, key ideas and details) address the CI Model's initial level of comprehension processes, constructing a microstructure of the text. Reading Anchor Standards 4–6 (cluster 2, craft and structure) address comprehension processes at the next level of the CI Model, constructing a macrostructure of the text. Reading Anchor Standards 7–9 (cluster 3, integration of knowledge and ideas) address comprehension processes at the final level of CI Model, integration to create a situation model.

This section presents three examples of CI theory–grounded comprehension lessons for the CCSS for reading literature. Although instruction in a single classroom would address comprehension processes at each level of the CI Model, the sample lessons provided in this chapter have been organized to represent one section of the three comprehension levels using CCSS ELA/Literacy Standards for each of the primary (K–2) grade levels.

- The first sample lesson, designed for kindergarten students, presents an example of the initial level of the CI Model, constructing a microstructure of the text.
- The second sample lesson, designed for 1st-grade students, presents an example of the second level of the CI Model, constructing a macrostructure of the text.
- The third sample lesson, designed for 2nd-grade students, presents an example of the final level of CI Model, integration to create a situation model.

The sample lessons correspond with the CI Model Lesson Framework presented in Figure 3.1. Each of the lessons uses one of the stories identified in the Appendix B of the CCSS for ELA/Literacy as exemplary literature.

CONSTRUCTING KNOWLEDGE WITH TEXT: A FOCUS ON THE MICROSTRUCTURE

Considering Text Selection and Complexity

Our kindergarten teacher, Ms. Claire, has selected a potential story to use as part of a unit about family celebrations, "Birthday Soup" from the book *Little Bear* (Minarik, 1957). This book is a Level 1 Beginning Reading book in the I Can Read book series. CCSS ELA/Literacy Standard 10 for reading literature in kindergarten is: Actively engage in group reading activities with purpose and understanding. Ms. Claire believes this book can be used successfully in a group reading, fits well with the theme of the

Figure 3.1. Construction–Integration (CI) Model Lesson Framework for Teaching CCSS Reading Anchor Standards

Step 1. Select Text and Evaluate Complexity (Standard 10)

Text _____

Genre _____

Theme/Topic _____

Difficulty (Lexile Bands) _____

Quantitative Supports (word length, word-meaning familiarity, sentence length, word frequency, cohesion devices explicitly used, etc.)

- _____
- _____
- _____

Qualitative Supports (illustrations, headings, typographic styles, graphic aids, photos, text structure, plot or topical complexity, language use [i.e., conventionality, clarity, etc.])

- _____
- _____
- _____

Quantitative Obstacles (word length, word-meaning familiarity, sentence length, word frequency, cohesion devices implicit, etc.)

- _____
- _____
- _____

Qualitative Obstacles (illustrations, headings, typographic styles, graphic aids, photos, text structure, plot or topical complexity, language use [i.e., conventionality, clarity, inferential load, etc.])

- _____
- _____
- _____

Reader–Task Considerations (*Reader:* purpose, motivation, background knowledge, experiences; *Task:* assignment or evidence to demonstrate comprehension, e.g., answering questions, graphic organizer, word meanings, etc.)

- _____
- _____
- _____

Step 2. Construction (Level 1)—Microstructure (Close Reading 1)

Reading Anchor Standard Category/Cluster 1—Key Ideas and Details

Select Reading Anchor Standards (1–3) _____

Select Comprehension Strategy Set (This may be a single or multiple strategy set):

- Single Strategy :
- Multiple Strategies:

Figure 3.1, *continued*

Step 3. Construction (Level 2)—Macrostructure (Close Reading 2)

Reading Anchor Standard Category/Cluster 2—Author's Craft and Structure
Select Reading Anchor Standards (4–6) _____
Select Comprehension Strategy Set (This may be a single or multiple strategy set):
- Single Strategy :
- Multiple Strategies:

Step 4. Integration (Level 1)—Situation Model (Additional Close Reading if needed)

Reading Anchor Standard Category/Cluster 3—Integration of Knowledge and Ideas
Select Reading Standards (7–9) _____
Select Comprehension Strategy Set (This may be a single or multiple strategy set):
- Single Strategy :
- Multiple Strategies:

Step 5. Integration (Level 2)—Merge Situation Model into World Knowledge (Close Reading if needed)

Reading Anchor Standard Category/Cluster 3—Integration of Knowledge and Ideas
Select Reading Standards (1–9) _____
Select Comprehension Strategy Set (This may be a single or multiple strategy set):
- Single Strategy :
- Multiple Strategies:

---

unit, presents an engaging topic for young children, and uses repetition of words and sentences to help promote successful monitored reading for some students. She checks the Lexile level of the book and finds it is rated as a 370L. There is no text complexity grade band presented in the CCSS ELA/Literacy for grades K–1; however, the Lexile rating is below the grade band for grades 2–3 of 450–725L. Ms. Claire decides this story is appropriate for use, with sufficient supports for students.

Ms. Claire examines the book more closely to determine potential supports and obstacles of the story (see Figure 3.1). She identifies the following items:

- *Quantitative Supports*—There are many high-frequency words, appropriate sentence length, repetition of some sentences and difficult words.
- *Qualitative Supports*—Illustrations match text presented; plot structure is easy to follow, with clear identification of the problem faced by the characters.

- *Quantitative Obstacles*—Difficult words include carrots, potatoes, and tomatoes, but they are used only on the second page of the story and are presented in a rhythmic pattern.
- *Qualitative Obstacles*—None noted.
- *Reader-Task Considerations*—Text fits well with the identified task and presents an engaging story.

Based on her examination of the text, Ms. Claire decides to include this story as one of the texts for the family celebrations unit.

Selecting Standards and Strategies

Ms. Claire first must select standards and comprehension strategies for the lesson. She uses Reading Anchor Standards for Literature 1–3 (cluster 1—key ideas and details) to identify grade-specific standards to help her students construct a microstructure of the text. Given the strong plot structure of the story, she selects Standard 3: With prompting and support, identify characters, settings, and major events in a story. Next, she considers comprehension strategies that will enable students to identify the characters, settings, and major events. Ms. Claire refers to the six comprehension strategies listed in the IES Practice Guide about comprehension instruction for primary-grade students for help with selecting a comprehension strategy (Shanahan et al., 2010). Briefly, these include: (1) activating prior knowledge or predicting; (2) questioning; (3) visualization; (4) monitoring, clarifying, or fix-up strategies; (5) inference; and (6) retelling. She decides to teach students how to ask and answer questions about the three components of story structure mentioned above. She will use a graphic organizer to help students with this task. Ms. Claire knows this task can be used with other stories and will prepare students for later lessons that address the macrostructure of stories. Her lesson (see Figure 3.2) will teach students how to ask and answer questions to identify the characters, settings, and major events in a story using explicit instruction, teacher think-alouds, and whole-class discussion.

Figure 3.2. Lesson 1: Supporting Construction of Microstructure

CCSS Anchor Standard: Key Ideas and Details #3 (Kindergarten)—With prompting and support, identify characters, settings, and major events in a story.
Materials: A big-book copy of *Little Bear* (Minarik, 1957) or a regular-size copy and a document camera, markers, large chart paper divided into three columns prepared as shown below.

Who?	Where?	What?

Lesson Objective/Explanation: (Teacher wording is in italics.) *We will learn how to ask and answer questions to help us better understand stories. We will be asking and answering the three questions shown on this chart: Who? Where? and What? As I read this story aloud to you, be thinking about these three questions: Who is the story about? Where is the story taking place? and What is happening in the story?*

Teacher Modeling:

1. Teacher reads aloud the story "Birthday Soup" from the book *Little Bear*.
2. *Did you listen carefully and think about Who, Where, and What? Let's read this story again and raise our hands when we hear a Who, Where, or What. As I read, I am going to ask myself Who, Where, and What about the story.* Teacher reads page 1 of the story and (as students raise their hands) presents a think-aloud about the Who presented on this page. Teacher explains that *the Who of a story is also called the characters* and explains the importance of characters for a story. Teacher also emphasizes that *when reading a story, asking and answering the question, "Who are the characters in the story?" will help us to better understand the story.* Teacher writes or draws the characters presented on page 1 of the story on the chart.
3. Teacher reads page 2 of the story and discusses the Where of the story and the first What of the story (in this case, the first What is the problem of the story). Teacher provides the label "setting" for the Where and the label "events" for the What. Teacher continues to write or draw the answers on the chart and discuss the importance of asking and answering these questions.
4. Teacher continues to read aloud and explain and discuss the Who, Where, and What of the story, articulating how use of the strategy of asking and answering questions about these three components increases understanding of the story. As students begin to understand the concept of asking and answering questions about the Who, Where, and What, teacher moves to guided practice.

Guided Practice (using the strategy with gradual release of responsibility):
Teacher draws students into collaborative use of the strategy of asking and answering

Figure 3.2. Lesson 1, *continued*

questions about these three components to better understand what is happening in the story. For example:

Initial Guided Practice—*As I read this next page, continue to listen carefully to this story and raise your hand when you hear an answer to a Who, Where, or What question.* Teacher continues reading. When a student raises his/her hand, teacher and student(s) discuss the Who, Where, or What, and teacher or student adds the answers to the chart.

Intermediate Guided Practice—*Continue to listen carefully to this story, asking yourself and answering Who, Where, or What questions. I'll stop at the end of each page and you can tell your reading partner your question and answer. We'll share our questions and answers with one another and add the answers to our chart.*

Independent Practice: Depending on the responsiveness of the students, independent practice of the strategy might be applied during this read-aloud or reserved for a subsequent read-aloud. Over time, independent practice of the strategy can progress to students completing a Who, Where, What Question/Answer Chart with a partner or individually. For example:

Independent Practice During This Read-Aloud—*Continue to listen carefully to this story, asking yourself and answering Who, Where, or What questions. When you hear an answer to a question, raise your hand and we'll draw or write the answer on our chart.*

Independent Practice During Subsequent Read-Alouds—*When you ask and answer a Who, Where, or What question, draw or write the answer on your partner Question/Answer chart.*

Independent Practice During Student Reading—When you ask and answer a Who, Where, or What question, write the page number of the story and draw or write the answer on your Question/Answer chart.

Lesson Conclusion: Teacher reviews with students the Who, Where, and What questions and answers, emphasizing how asking and answering these questions has helped to increase understanding of the story.

This first sample lesson was designed to help students construct a microstructure (CI Model Step 2) of the story "Birthday Soup" from the book *Little Bear* (Minarik, 1957). This lesson has prepared students to delve more deeply into the next levels of the Construction–Integration Model: the craft and structure of this story (CI Model Step 3) and the integration of knowledge and ideas from this story into their world knowledge (CI Model Steps 4 and 5). Thus, Ms. Claire will teach additional lessons based on the Construction–Integration Model using this story to build students' comprehension skills. Over time, students will grow not only in comprehension skills, but in foundational reading skills as they experience repeated exposure to the high-frequency words and other features of this story and similar literature (Duke et al., 2011). Table 3.1 provides suggestions for CI-based reading comprehension lessons using the story "Birthday Soup" to teach CCSS ELA/Literacy

Table 3.1. Lesson Suggestions Using the Story "Birthday Soup"

"Birthday Soup" from the book *Little Bear* by Else Holmelund Minarik (1957)

CCSS ELA/Literacy Reading Standards for Literature 1–9, Kindergarten

		Key Ideas and Details
Microstructure	Standard 1	With prompting and support, ask and answer questions about key details in a text. *Teaching Suggestion:* Demonstrate for students how to ask and answer questions about: (a) why Little Bear decides to make birthday soup; (b) what Little Bear does to make birthday soup; (c) who comes to eat his birthday soup; and (d) who surprises Little Bear. Encourage students to ask and answer questions of their own.
	Standard 2	With prompting and support, retell familiar stories, including key details. *Teaching Suggestion:* Demonstrate for students how to retell the story of "Birthday Soup" using the key details identified in Standard 1. Have students draw a series of pictures to retell the story in a comic strip frame format. Have students cut apart the pictures, reorder them, and retell the story to others.
	Standard 3	**With prompting and support, identify characters, settings, and major events in a story.** *Teaching Suggestion:* Use Sample Lesson 1.
		Craft and Structure
Macrostructure	Standard 4	Ask and answer questions about unknown words in text. *Teaching Suggestion:* Demonstrate for students what to do for an unknown word in a text. Encourage students to use the techniques shared. (Students are likely to know the meaning of all the words in the story "Birthday Soup.")
	Standard 5	Recognize common types of texts (e.g., storybooks, poems). *Teaching Suggestion:* Show students how the book *Little Bear* is a collection of short stories. Point out the title of the book and the titles of each of the stories. Have students identify other books that are a collection of short stories.
	Standard 6	With prompting and support, name the author and illustrator of a story and define the role of each in telling the story. *Teaching Suggestion:* Identify the author and illustrator of the book *Little Bear*. Discuss how these two people worked together to create several children's books. Compare some of these books with *Little Bear*. Explain how the illustrator, Maurice Sendak (1963), wrote and illustrated his own stories such as those in *Where the Wild Things Are*.

Table 3.1. *Continued*

Integration of Knowledge and Ideas

Integration	Standard 7	With prompting and support, describe the relationship between illustrations and the story in which they appear (e.g., what moment in a story an illustration depicts). *Teaching Suggestion:* Take students on a "picture walk" through the story "Birthday Soup." Identify important events that do not have an illustration and draw illustrations for those events.
	Standard 8	(Not applicable to literature.)
	Standard 9	With prompting and support, compare and contrast the adventures and experiences of characters in familiar stories. *Teaching Suggestion:* Use the book *Five Little Monkeys Bake a Birthday Cake* by Eileen Christelow (2004) to make these comparisons. Both this book and "Birthday Soup" involve creating food for birthday events, but the techniques for making the food are very different.

Reading Standards for Literature 1–9 at the kindergarten level (the bolded lesson is Sample Lesson 1).

CONSTRUCTING KNOWLEDGE WITH TEXT: A FOCUS ON THE MACROSTRUCTURE

Considering Text Selection and Complexity

Mr. Dereik, a 1st-grade teacher, selected the story "The Garden" from the book *Frog and Toad Together* (Lobel, 1971b) as part of a unit about the theme of perseverance. This book is a Level 2 Beginning Reading book in the I Can Read book series. CCSS ELA/Literacy Standard 10 for Reading Literature in 1st grade is: With prompting and support, read prose and poetry of appropriate complexity for grade 1. Mr. Dereik knows this book is listed as exemplary literature in Appendix B of the CCSS ELA/Literacy. However, before deciding to use this book, he followed the CI Model Lesson Framework (presented in Figure 3.1) to analyze the complexity of this book. The Lexile rating of this book is 330L. Mr. Dereik realizes that although there is no text complexity grade band presented in the CCSS ELA/Literacy for grades K–1, the rating for this book is below the Lexile grade band for grades 2–3 of 450–725L.

In preparation for instruction, Mr. Dereik examined the book more closely to identify potential supports and obstacles of the story and noted the following items:

- *Quantitative Supports*—Many high-frequency words, nice variety of sentence length.
- *Qualitative Supports*—Engaging, humorous story, illustrations match text presented, easy-to-follow plot structure, limited to two characters.
- *Quantitative Obstacles*—Potentially difficult words limited to the word frightened.
- *Qualitative Obstacles*—None noted.
- *Reader–Task Considerations*—Text fits well with the identified theme, allows for possible extensions, is likely to be enjoyable to students.

Based on his examination of the text, Mr. Dereik determined this book suitable for his purposes and currently is using the book for comprehension instruction. Mr. Dereik has already used this book with comprehension instruction for the first level of textbase processing of the CI Model (Step 2), constructing a microstructure, and is ready to begin instruction for the second level of textbase processing (Step 3), constructing a macrostructure of the text. (Lesson 1 presented an example of a lesson for constructing a microstructure.)

Selecting Standards and Strategies

Mr. Dereik looks at Reading Standards for Literature 4–6 (cluster 2—craft and structure) to identify a grade-specific standard to help his students construct a macrostructure of the text. He selects standard 4: Identify words and phrases in stories or poems that suggest feelings or appeal to the senses. Mr. Dereik recognizes that this particular story is rich with phrases that express the thoughts and feelings of the two characters, Frog and Toad. Next, he considers comprehension strategies that will fit with this reading standard and help students to understand how these words and phrases suggesting feelings are important to gaining a better understanding of the story. Mr. Dereik selects the comprehension strategies of activating background knowledge and of drawing inferences; specifically, he will focus on what students can learn about the story from these phrases that present feelings. He will use explicit instruction, teacher think-alouds, and discussion to teach this lesson (see Figure 3.3).

Figure 3.3. Lesson 2: Supporting Construction of Macrostructure to Complete Text-base

---

CCSS Anchor Standard: Craft and Structure #4 (1st Grade)—Identify words and phrases in stories or poems that suggest feelings or appeal to the senses.

Materials: Copies of the book *Frog and Toad Together* (Lobel, 1971b) for each student and teacher, Post-it highlighter flags for teacher and each student.

Lesson Objective/Explanation: (Teacher wording is in italics.) *We will learn how to identify words and phrases that the author has included in a story to describe thoughts and feelings of the characters. When we read words or sentences that tell about how a character is thinking or feeling, we will put a highlighter tape on the words or sentence. We will discuss how these words and phrases help us to better understand the story.*

Teacher Modeling:

1. Teacher reads page 1 of the story and shares a think-aloud: *These sentences show how a character is thinking or feeling. I'll put highlighter tape by the sentence. The author wrote this sentence to help us understand how Frog feels about growing a garden. Frog thinks growing a garden is hard work. I agree with Frog. I have grown a garden and it takes many steps. First, I have to prepare the soil . . . etc. I think the author had Frog tell Toad that growing a garden is hard work because, as we have learned from other stories about these two characters, Toad sometimes has difficulty finishing a task.*

2. Teacher reads page 2 of the story and shares a think-aloud: *These are more sentences the author has included to help us understand the characters' thoughts and feelings. I'll put highlighter tape by these sentences. When Toad asks a question about how long it will take for a garden to grow, it hints at his impatience. Again, from my background knowledge about growing a garden, it takes about 10 days for the seeds to start growing. I don't think Frog's understanding of how long it takes a garden to grow is the same as Toad's.*

3. Teacher continues reading the story and sharing think-alouds about words or phrases the author has included in the story to indicate the characters' feelings and thoughts. Teacher shares relevant background knowledge and inferences about the words or phrases to increase understanding of the macrostructure of the story. As students begin to understand these concepts, teacher moves to guided practice.

Guided Practice (using the strategy with gradual release of responsibility): Teacher draws students into collaborative use of identifying words and phrases that describe thoughts and feelings of the characters through activating background knowledge and drawing inferences. For example:

Initial Guided Practice—*Let's read this next page together to identify words or sentences that describe the characters' feelings and thoughts. When we read a sentence that we think tells about how a character is feeling or what a character is thinking, we will put high-lighter tape by the sentence.* During the initial guided practice, the teacher continues to model putting the highlighter tape in his/her book as students put highlighter tape in their books. Teacher reads the text, emphasizing and discussing with students the words and phrases the author has included in the story to indicate the characters' feelings and thoughts. Teacher shares his/her think-alouds, presenting relevant background knowledge and inferences to increase understanding of the macrostructure of the story. The words and phrases that indicate feelings and thoughts are discussed one-by-one as they are presented in the text.

Figure 3.3. Lesson 2, *continued*

Intermediate Guided Practice—During the intermediate guided practice, the teacher allocates more responsibility to the students. Rather than discussing the words and phrases one-by-one as they are presented in the text, the teacher reads aloud a page (or a few pages) and has students place the highlighter tape during the read-aloud (the teacher is not placing highlighter tape in his/her copy at this point). The teacher and students discuss the words or phrases after every page (or few pages). The amount of text read before a discussion takes place is manipulated to shift increasing responsibility to the students.

Independent Practice: For these 1st-grade students, independent practice will likely occur during this same lesson. Students are already familiar with the story due to the previous lesson on the story's microstructure. Thus, independent practice will move to having the students read section of the text (aloud to themselves or with a partner) and place the highlighter tape on the words and phrases that describe thoughts and feelings of the characters. Again, the amount of text that students are instructed to read before a discussion takes place can be manipulated to distribute more or less responsibility to the students.

Lesson Conclusion: Teacher reviews with students the importance of the words and phrases the author has included in the story to describe thoughts and feelings of the characters. Teacher emphasizes that, combined with the author's words, thinking about personal experiences can help readers infer how a character is feeling.

This second sample lesson was designed to help students construct a macrostructure (CI Model Step 3) of the story "The Garden" from the book *Frog and Toad Together* (Lobel, 1971b). This lesson has prepared students for Mr. Dereik's upcoming lessons grounded in the next level of the Construction–Integration Model: integration of knowledge and ideas from this story into their world knowledge (CI Model Steps 4 and 5). Table 3.2 provides suggestions for CI theory–grounded reading comprehension lessons using the story "The Garden" for CCSS ELA/Literacy Reading Standards for Literature 1–9 at the 1st-grade level (the bolded lesson is Sample Lesson 2).

INTEGRATING TEXT KNOWLEDGE WITH BACKGROUND KNOWLEDGE: BUILDING A SITUATION MODEL

Considering Text Selection and Complexity

In this final example of CI theory–based comprehension lessons for the CCSS ELA Standards for Reading Literature, Ms. Laurens has been using the story "Henry and Mudge" from the book *Henry and Mudge: The First Book of Their Adventures* (Rylant, 1987) with her 2nd-grade

Table 3.2. Lesson Suggestions Using the Story "The Garden"

"The Garden" from the book *Frog and Toad Together* (Lobel, 1971b)

CCSS. ELA/Literacy Reading Standards for Literature 1–9, 1st Grade

		Key Ideas and Details
Microstructure	Standard 1	Ask and answer questions about key details in a text. *Teaching Suggestion:* Demonstrate for students how to ask and answer questions about: (a) why Toad decides to plant a garden; (b) how Toad tries to make his garden grow; and (c) what finally happens to Toad's garden. Encourage students to ask and answer questions of their own.
	Standard 2	Retell stories, including key details, and demonstrate understanding of their central message or lesson. *Teaching Suggestion:* Demonstrate for students how to retell the story of "The Garden" using the key details identified in Standard 1. Have students act out the story in sequential order.
	Standard 3	Describe characters, settings, and major events in a story, using key details. *Teaching Suggestion:* Develop a character analysis of Frog and Toad. Discuss the similarities and differences of the gardening styles, work ethics, and other characteristics of these two characters.
		Craft and Structure
Macrostructure	**Standard 4**	**Identify words and phrases in stories or poems that suggest feelings or appeal to the senses.** *Teaching Suggestion:* Use Sample Lesson 2.
	Standard 5	Explain major differences between books that tell stories and books that give information, drawing on a wide reading of a range of text types. *Teaching Suggestion:* Compare the book *Frog and Toad Together* with the book *Frogs!* (Carney, 2009). Discuss with students the differences between the two books and the differences in the portrayal of frogs.
	Standard 6	Identify who is telling the story at various points in a text. *Teaching Suggestion:* Create simple puppets for the characters of Frog and Toad. Have students present a puppet show as the teacher or students read the story aloud. Discuss how the author used dialogue to present the story.

students. This book is a Level 2 reader in the Ready to Read series. CCSS ELA/Literacy Standard 10 for Reading Literature in 2nd grade is: By the end of the year, read and comprehend literature, including stories and poetry, in the grades 2–3 text complexity band proficiently, with scaffolding as needed at the high end of the range. Similar to the other books used in

Table 3.2, *continued*

		Integration of Knowledge and Ideas
Integration	Standard 7	Use illustrations and details in a story to describe its characters, setting, or events. *Teaching Suggestion:* Have students use the illustrations to retell the story. Identify key details of the story and discuss how the illustrations add or detract from the descriptions presented.
	Standard 8	(Not applicable to literature.)
	Standard 9	Compare and contrast the adventures and experiences of characters in stories. *Teaching Suggestion:* Compare the story "The Garden" with the next story in the book, "Cookies." Discuss the leadership and responsibility roles of Frog and Toad in these two short stories.

the sample lessons in this chapter, this book is listed as a text exemplar for literature in Appendix B of the CCSS ELA/Literacy. Prior to beginning instruction with this book, Ms. Laurens analyzed the complexity of the book using the CI Model Lesson Framework (presented in Figure 3.1). The text complexity Lexile grade band for grades 2–3 is 450–725L. The Lexile rating of *Henry and Mudge: The First Book of Their Adventures* is 460L.

Based on her examination, Ms. Laurens deemed the book suitable for her purposes for potential supports and obstacles of the story, which identified the following items:

- *Quantitative Supports*—Many high-frequency words, some compound sentences, no potentially difficult words noted.
- *Qualitative Supports*—Illustrations match text presented, story is limited to two characters.
- *Quantitative Obstacles*—Sentence length (final sentence has 33 words), poetic style of writing for some sentences.
- *Qualitative Obstacles*—Several sentences begin with the word "and."
- *Reader-Task Considerations*—This is the final story in the book, and understanding of this story is dependent on the previous stories in the book.

Ms. Laurens has already used this book with comprehension instruction for the first and second levels of textbase processing of the CI Model, constructing a microstructure and macrostructure of the text to form a textbase. (Lessons 1 and 2 presented previously in this chapter provide examples of lessons for constructing a textbase.) Thus, students are already familiar with this story and are prepared for the next level of the CI Model, creating a situation model of the text (Steps 4 and 5 in the CI Model Lesson Framework presented in Figure 3.1.) Duke et al. (2011) defined a situation model as the "coherent mental representation of the events, actions, and conditions in the text that represent the integration of the text base with relevant prior knowledge from readers' store of knowledge in long-term memory" (p. 54).

Selecting Standards and Strategies

Ms. Laurens identifies a grade-specific standard from Reading Standards for Literature 7–9 (cluster 3—integration of knowledge and ideas) to help her students create and integrate a situation model. She selects Standard 7: Use information gained from the illustrations and words in a print or digital text to demonstrate understanding of its characters, setting, or plot. As this story describes the relationship of Henry and Mudge, Ms. Laurens will focus specifically on increasing students' understanding of the characters. She plans to have students use the comprehension strategies of retelling and visualization to create a situation model from the textbase. She will use explicit instruction, teacher think-alouds, and discussion to teach this lesson (see Figure 3.4). As this is the final story in this book, she will draw on students' knowledge across each of the short stories presented in this book to help students comprehend this concluding story and to demonstrate how examining the relationship of characters can be applied to reading other narrative texts.

This third sample lesson was designed to help students build and merge a situation into their world knowledge (CI Model Steps 4 and 5) using the story "Henry and Mudge" from the book *Henry and Mudge: The First Book of Their Adventures* (Rylant, 1987). This lesson completed the final step of the Construction–Integration Model with this story. However, the teacher may continue to use this story (as desired) or draw from students' knowledge of this story for future lessons (such as comparisons of characters). Table 3.3 provides suggestions for CI theory–grounded reading comprehension lessons using the story "Henry and Mudge" for CCSS ELA/Literacy Reading Standards for Literature 1–9 at the 2nd-grade level (the bolded lesson is Sample Lesson 3).

Figure 3.4. Lesson 3: Supporting Creation of a Situation Model

CCSS Anchor Standard: Integration of Knowledge and Ideas #7 (2nd Grade)—Use information gained from the illustrations and words in a print or digital text to demonstrate understanding of its characters, setting, or plot.

Materials: Copies of the book *Henry and Mudge: The First Book of Their Adventures* (Rylant, 1987) for each student and teacher, blank drawing paper, drawing media (colored pencils, crayons, etc.).

Lesson Objective/Explanation: (Teacher wording is in italics.) *We have already read this last story in our* Henry and Mudge *book. Today, we will be rereading parts of this story and other stories in this book, thinking about the descriptions in the stories, and looking at the illustrations to help us analyze the relationship of the two main characters. An important part of any story is the development of the characters.*

Teacher Modeling:

1. Teacher reads page 1 of the story and shares a think-aloud: *When I read these words and look at the picture, I can tell that Henry and Mudge really care about each other. They like to see each other first thing in the morning. When I think about the story in this book that describes when Mudge was lost (retell a portion of the story, including a visualization), I understand even more about <u>why</u> these two characters are so happy to see each other first thing in the morning. Retelling parts of the stories help me to remember and visualize the events that have helped make these two characters best friends.*

2. Teacher shares another reread, retell, and visualization about the relationship of the two characters. For example: *Another part of the story that helps me to think about the closeness of the two characters are these sentences on page 5.* (Teacher reads page 5 of the story.) *I can picture in my mind when Mudge was lost and how frightening that was* (teacher retells a portion of the story, including visualizations).

3. Teacher continues sharing rereads, retells, and visualizations about how the illustrations and sentences help to increase the reader's understanding of the relationship of Henry and Mudge in building a situation model of the importance of character development. As students begin to understand this concept, teacher moves to guided practice.

Guided Practice (using the strategy with gradual release of responsibility):
Teacher draws students into collaborative use of rereading, retelling, and visualizing about the relationship of the two characters. For example:
Initial Guided Practice—*Another part that helps me understand the relationship of these characters is on page 6* (Teacher reads page 6). *What do you visualize when you hear that sentence and how does that help you to understand the relationship of Henry and Mudge?*
During the initial guided practice, the teacher continues to direct students to sections of text or illustrations and elicits students' visualizations and retells about the sections to help students build a situation model of the characters and their relationship.
Intermediate Guided Practice—During the intermediate guided practice, the teacher allocates more responsibility to the students by having students identify sections of text or illustrations and continues guiding the discussion of the retelling and visualization about the characters.

Figure 3.4. Lesson 3, *continued*

Independent Practice: This lesson includes independent practice. Each student will scan through the book to identify a section of text or an illustration that helps him/her understand the relationship of the two main characters. Each student will draw a visualization of his/her selection. Students will meet in small groups to share the visualizations, retell the sections, and discuss how the selected sections increased their understanding of the relationship of Henry and Mudge.

Lesson Conclusion: Teacher reiterates the importance of character development for stories (literature). Teacher reviews with students how thinking carefully about the descriptions and the illustrations can increase understanding of the story's characters.

Table 3.3. Lesson Suggestions Using the Story "Henry and Mudge"

"Henry and Mudge" from the book *Henry and Mudge: The First Book of Their Adventures* (Rylant, 1987)

CCSS. ELA/Literacy Reading Standards for Literature 1–9, 2nd Grade

		Key Ideas and Details
Microstructure	Standard 1	Ask and answer such questions as who, what, where, when, why, and how to demonstrate understanding of key details in a text.
		Teaching Suggestion: Expand the graphic organizer presented in Sample Lesson 1 to include these additional questions. Model and discuss with students how to ask and answer these questions using words and passages from the text.
	Standard 2	Recount stories, including fables and folktales from diverse cultures, and determine their central message, lesson, or moral.
		Teaching Suggestion: With students, create a list of lessons that could be learned from this story. Identify the words or phrases that present these lessons.
	Standard 3	Describe how characters in a story respond to major events and challenges.
		Teaching Suggestion: Create a timeline of the events in this story. Describe how Henry and Mudge responded to each event.

Table 3.3, *continued*

		Craft and Structure
Macrostructure	Standard 4	Describe how words and phrases (e.g., regular beats, alliteration, rhymes, repeated lines) supply rhythm and meaning in a story, poem, or song. *Teaching Suggestion:* Analyze the author's use of sentence structure (e.g., sentences that begin with the word *and*), the use of poetry-like stanzas on some pages, etc.
	Standard 5	Describe the overall structure of a story, including describing how the beginning introduces the story and the ending concludes the action. *Teaching Suggestion:* Complete a story map for the book *Henry and Mudge: The First Book of Their Adventures.* Discuss how the short stories in this collection work together to create an overall story structure.
	Standard 6	Acknowledge differences in the points of view of characters, including by speaking in a different voice for each character when reading dialogue aloud. *Teaching Suggestion:* Compare Henry's view with his parents' view about the importance of a pet. Identify the pros and cons of different types of dogs for a pet (e.g., large dogs, small dogs, etc.). Discuss Henry's choice and decide whether it was a good fit for his family.
Integration		Integration of Knowledge and Ideas
	Standard 7	**Use information gained from the illustrations and words in a print or digital text to demonstrate understanding of its characters, setting, or plot.** *Teaching Suggestion:* Use Sample Lesson 3.
	Standard 8	(Not applicable to literature.)
	Standard 9	Compare and contrast two or more versions of the same story (e.g., Cinderella stories) by different authors or from different cultures. *Teaching Suggestion:* This standard is not applicable to this story

THE BENEFITS OF THE CI MODEL FOR STANDARDS-BASED LITERATURE INSTRUCTION

The use of literature for teaching reading comprehension is an important staple in the primary grades. The Construction–Integration Model of Text Comprehension necessitates the reading and rereading of texts for targeted, specific purposes. Students analyze texts from a variety of perspectives to create a microstructure, macrostructure, and situation model. Students examine the phrases, sentences, structure, illustrations, and other literary devices. Literature brings the reader and the text "close together" through personal involvement, as primary-grade students can pay close attention to relevant experiences and thoughts, to the responses and interpretations of the teacher and other students, and to the interactions among these elements (Beers & Probst, 2012). The philosopher Sir Francis Bacon wrote, "Some books are to be tasted, others to be swallowed, and some few to be chewed and digested" (Scott, 1908, p. 234). Fortunately, children's literature provides a delightful assortment of quality stories and poems to be "chewed and digested" as we teach children the strategies to access, consider, and evaluate key ideas and details, craft and structure, and to integrate knowledge and ideas.

CHAPTER 4

Designing Instruction to Teach Informational Text

CHAPTER OVERVIEW

In the previous chapter, we learned about strategies and lessons designed to increase student comprehension of literature books using Kintsch's CI Model of Text comprehension as a framework. In this chapter, we will highlight strategies and comprehension lessons designed to strengthen Pre-K–3 comprehension of informational texts using the same framework.

Comprehension of Informational Text

Research has demonstrated that elementary students tend to comprehend narrative text more easily than they do informational text (Berkowitz & Taylor, 1981; Langer, Applebee, Mullis, & Foertsch, 1990; Olson, 1985). This is due mostly to the different reading skills needed to comprehend informational text and the lack of exposure young children have to reading informational texts (Duke, 2000). Researchers have long noted that the "reading slump" that occurs in student reading achievement around 4th grade has been attributed largely to the inability of students to read informational text proficiently (Chall, Jacobs, & Baldwin, 1990; Duke, Halliday, & Roberts, 2013). The National Assessment of Educational Progress Reading Report Card (NAEP, 2011) revealed that large numbers of elementary school children struggle to read informational text proficiently, especially those students who are at-risk, low-income, and minority students. This is of grave concern as informational text becomes increasingly prominent and important to success in today's society. Unfortunately, Duke (2002) reported that up to 44 million adults in the United States struggle to read and comprehend informational texts proficiently, making it difficult for them to be successful in college or in their career.

Text Structure of Informational texts

Informational texts are structured very differently than literature and narrative texts, and therefore require an emphasis on text features, an understanding of how to read content-specific information, as well as the use of
multiple close readings to ensure that students understand the information that is presented in the informational text format. See Table 4.1 for
a listing of the text structures unique to informational text.

Most informational texts are organized around a specific topic in
a hierarchical or structural manner (Kintsch & van Dijk, 1978; Meyer,
1975), thus allowing the reader to decode and retrieve information in
an organized fashion. However, research has demonstrated that children
need explicit instruction to assist them in learning how to use these structures and features (Duke et al., 2011; Pearson & Fielding, 1991) to make
meaning and understand text. The focus of this chapter will be to demonstrate for teachers not only how to design comprehension instruction
for young children using the CCSS but how to incorporate and infuse
Kintsch's theory and model of comprehension into this comprehension
instruction as well.

SETTING THE STAGE FOR COMPREHENSION INSTRUCTION
OF INFORMATIONAL TEXTS

As students begin to decode words and phrases, they simultaneously are
building skills needed to comprehend what they are reading. Reading
comprehension instruction at school is an ideal place to learn these skills
as the classroom provides a setting where vibrant social interaction and
exchange can take place between a student and the teacher and among
students. Together, through joint discussions rich with questioning and
close readings, students and teachers jointly and independently can construct and integrate meaning. However, for this to take place, the teacher
needs first to understand the text that is being read, to recognize text
features and text structures within the text that will enable comprehension, and to know how to model ideal thinking and scaffold skills that will
enable students to develop deeper comprehension.

The CSSS, with their 10 standards for comprehension of literature,
balanced with the 10 standards for comprehension of informational
text, place a much stronger emphasis on informational text than ever
before—especially in the early elementary grades. It is recommended in

Table 4.1. Informational text Structures

Informational Text Structure	Attributes	Signal Words
Description	The key point or main idea is supported by details and/or examples	for example, is, are, have, has, another kind of, most important, described as
Sequence	The text presents a main idea that follows a particular sequence or process	first, second, next, then, finally, before, when, after, until, in the end
Problem/Solution	When a problem or question is posed and considered followed by a solution or answer	the question is, the problem is, therefore, if . . . then
Cause/Effect	The details within the text explain and identify the cause(s) followed by the effects of this cause	because of, since, therefore, as a result, thus, hence
Compare/Contrast	When one or two main ideas or concepts are compared for similarities and contrasted to determine differences	in contrast, similarly, on the other hand, compared with, different from, same as

these reading standards that young students listen to or read a balance (a 50/50 proportion) of informational text and literature. Many elementary school teachers are scrambling to fill their classroom shelves with more informational texts as their bookshelves and their classroom read-aloud times typically have featured literature books. Thus, we have the following recommendations for gathering exemplar informational texts to be used with young children:

First, refer to Standard 10 on text complexity in the grade level that you are teaching to understand how text complexity is addressed at that grade level. Questions to consider: What books are considered complex for my students? How will I support and scaffold learning with these complex texts? How will I merge the content-area topics of social studies and science into my literacy instruction and in my classroom library? What background knowledge do my students bring to these subjects, ideas, and concepts? What knowledge might need to be taught or included?

Second, select informational texts where the title provides a clear indication of what the book is about and the text structure being used.

Third, select informational texts in which only one text structure has been used consistently throughout the book. The five text structures are description, sequence, cause–effect, compare–contrast, and problem–solution (or sometimes question–answer).

These same criteria may not be necessary for informational texts that are used for pleasure reading or classroom read-alouds with young children. In time, students will be expected to read informational texts that are more complex and/or that incorporate mixed text structures, but exemplar texts should be used early on so young children can develop an understanding of these features and structures. With experience, young children can learn to navigate informational text before moving on to more complex informational text that demands much more of the reader and where the author does not provide structural supports.

TEACHING CCSS READING STANDARDS FOR INFORMATIONAL TEXT

As all teachers are expected to teach the comprehension skills outlined in the CCSS and individual state standards, this section will present a sample lesson to show how to incorporate CI theory into reading comprehension instruction with informational text. To begin, the teacher first must select a text that will help teach the skill or standard for comprehension of informational text. The teacher needs to attend to Anchor Standard 10 of the reading standards to ensure the correct *range of reading and level of text complexity* in the book selected.

Text Complexity and Range

There are four criteria the teacher considers when selecting texts that will address text complexity and range:

- Interest for students
- The Goldilocks principle
- Genre
- Quality

First and foremost, the teacher needs to consider how interesting to students the content or material presented in the text really is. In these CCSS comprehension lessons, students will be expected to read a book multiple times to gain new meaning and understanding each time. In the lesson sample presented below, Mrs. Williams selects *Autumn* (Berger & Berger, 2004) for her kindergarten comprehension lesson because of the rich vocabulary words used and the complex thoughts and ideas expressed by the authors. While this particular book uses simple sentences to portray information, the authors use plenty of terms to assist students in developing a greater vocabulary, and plenty of concepts and ideas that can be discussed with each close reading. The text complexity of this particular book provides fertile ground for some deep discussions between teacher and students. For example, the word *autumn* itself will need to be discussed with students, as they may be more familiar with the term *fall* associated with this season. Other terms or concepts used and referenced in this book that can provide excellent opportunities for rich discussion include the following: the concept of hibernation, the concept of storing food for winter, what the word *ripe* means, what the word *cocoon* means, what the word *equinox* means, what makes leaves change color and fall to the ground, the harvest, what makes days shorter and cooler, the migration of geese, and so on. One can see that a simple informational text geared for kindergarten readers can simultaneously be an example of text complexity with its richness and possibility.

Second, the teacher needs to consider the Goldilocks principle. Is the book too easy? Too hard? Or just right? Students need a challenge level that is just right. The Lexile rating for *Autumn* is 325L, which puts it at a 1st-grade level and within the Lexile level stretch bandwidth suggested by the CCSS. Thus, not all the kindergarten students will be able to read the text independently, but the simple sentences used (either subject–verb or subject-verb–adverb/noun) make it easier for beginning readers to follow along and comprehend.

Third, the teacher needs to consider the genre of the text. As this lesson is designed to teach the comprehension of informational text, that type of text was selected. Mrs. Williams needs to remember that student exposure to informational text thus far may be very limited, so intentional modeling and scaffolding of reading and understanding will be necessary with this type of text.

Finally, the teacher needs to consider the qualitative aspects provided by the author. In *Autumn*, the authors employ the following qualitative aspects to support student comprehension: photographs, callouts with additional information, and a clearly identifiable text structure (in this case, descriptive.)

A Focus on the Microstructure

As fall is approaching, Mrs. Williams selects the book *Autumn* (Berger & Berger, 2004) to read with a small group of kindergarten students. She selected this informational text for the purpose of helping these young children develop reading comprehension skills as outlined in the CCSS and listed under key ideas and details. She decides to focus on Standard 2: With prompting and support, identify the main topic and retell key details of a text. She selects the *retelling* comprehension strategy to assist her in this lesson because it aligns well with this standard.

In reading the book *Autumn*, the students in this group must use the illustrations and symbols on the pages to make sense of what they read, and they need to be able to decode the words. Even if Mrs. Williams reads the story aloud first, her students will still need to link the decoded words, phrases, and sentences in working memory to word meanings, images, and/or experiences stored in their background knowledge. Building a microstructure requires the reader to understand what the words and phrases mean and not simply decode letters and sounds to create words.

The following lesson (see Figure 4.1) was designed by Mrs. Williams to assist students in constructing a microstructure of this information-al text to further strengthen students' understanding of word meanings and to build their linguistic background knowledge. Explicit instruction provides a great way to model, scaffold, and support the construction of the microstructure, and to identify the main ideas and retell key details from the text. Standard 2 involves two distinct skills (identifying the main idea and retelling key details from the text). Combining both of these skills into one lesson can be a lot for a kindergartner, so the teacher can easily break standards and skills into smaller learning chunks whenever necessary. This is especially important when designing lessons to teach the CCSS comprehension standards with young children.

This particular lesson designed to build the microstructure of the *Autumn* informational text is now complete, but Mrs. Williams will still have work to do and lessons to teach that will continue to support students in building a microstructure with this text. Teaching other key ideas and details standards (Standards 1–3) will require additional close readings of the text, with each lesson emphasizing a different aspect of the text. Additionally, Mrs. Williams will need to teach more lessons that will re-quire multiple close readings of the book *Autumn* with an emphasis this time on skills described in the craft and structure standards (Standards 4–6 of the CCSS for the comprehension of informational text). These

Figure 4.1. Lesson 1—Supporting Construction of Microstructure

CCSS Anchor Standard: Key Ideas and Details #2 (Kindergarten)—With prompting and support, identify the main topic and retell key details of a text. (This lesson will focus only on *retelling key details* of a text.)

Materials: A copy of *Autumn* (Berger & Berger, 2004) for each student and teacher, large butcher paper with circle drawn around the word AUTUMN, markers.

Lesson Objective/Explanation: (Teacher wording is in italics.) *Today we are going to practice sharing ideas we read about in books. Thinking about what we are reading and sharing these ideas with others is one way to help us understand what we are reading.* **Teacher Modeling:** (Teacher reads the book *Autumn* aloud to students.) *We just read this book aloud together about the season autumn. I'm going to look back over the book and pay attention to what I see and read to help me remember the details I learned about autumn. We write down what we learn about autumn from reading this book on this chart to help us remember.* (Teacher points to the chart with the big circle and reads "autumn" written in the middle of the circle.) *I read the first page. This sentence reminds me what the book is about.* (Teacher points to the word "autumn" written in the middle of the circle.) *Let me keep reading to see if I can find some information about autumn. Now I read the second page. Hmmm. I'm going to write about the leaves falling on my chart so I don't forget.* (Teacher draws a line coming from the circle and writes: Leaves fall in autumn.) *Writing this on the chart is retelling or recording what I read. In the picture, I can see lots of leaves on the ground. I have seen leaves fall on the ground in autumn. It is usually windy and that's what makes the leaves fall. Then, I read the next page. It talks about the wind blowing. Oh! I just said that. I need to record this on my paper too. It is windy in autumn. I can see the wind blowing the dandelion seeds in this picture.* (In this think-aloud, the teacher is demonstrating for students how to use words and the pictures to help create a microstructure of this text.)

Guided Practice (Scaffolding): (Scaffolding means the teacher participates along with students in retelling key details from the text. The teacher can hold back as the students gain skill and confidence.) *Now, let's do a few pages together. We are going to read the next page and look at the picture to help us figure out what other details I should add to our chart about autumn.* (Teacher reads the next page or has a student read the page.) *Wow! Some plants do grow big. What plant is in the picture?* (Student responds, "A pumpkin.") *That's right. It is a pumpkin. I've seen lots of pumpkins in autumn, have you? Let's share this or retell what we learned on our chart: Plants grow big. Has anyone seen a plant grow big? Now let's read the next page.* Another student reads about the farmer picking the plants. *Oh wow! That is something else we can add to our chart about autumn: Farmers need to pick the plants. Do you see any plants in this picture that are being picked by the farmer? What kind of plant is it?* (The teacher is demonstrating how the photographs can provide information as well as the words. The teacher reads the next page and asks another pair of students to retell the information they learn about autumn after the reading.) Students read about how the daylight hours are getting less and less. *Hmmm. I wonder what that means. How can we retell this or share what we just read?* (Students share ideas.) *I would agree. The days get shorter because the sun goes down earlier and so it gets dark sooner. Let's add this to the chart as well. How can we*

Figure 4.1, *continued*

retell or share what we learned on this page? (Students respond and teacher adds "Days are getting shorter" to the chart.)

Independent Practice (Gradual Release): *Okay. You are now ready to read a few pages on your own and see if you can figure out what the author is telling us about autumn. Be sure to use the words and the pictures to help make sense of what you read.* (The teacher stays right with the students to provide support, if needed, and to determine whether the students are able to do the skill independently. There are eight more pages in this book. The teacher can assign students to read a certain number of pages or read the remaining pages to the students, but should be sure to have the students retell or share the key details found on these pages. The teacher should be sure students can do this skill independently before moving on to the next standard. It may be necessary to do more than one lesson on this standard using a different informational text.)
Assessment: The teacher reviews what was recorded on the chart about the details students identified from the informational text describing autumn. The teacher encourages students at the end of the lesson to share in their own words the key details they can remember about the text, using the book or the poster as a guide. This will allow the teacher to determine whether students need further assistance in retelling details or whether they can do this skill independently.

additional lessons will help students to build an overall viewpoint of the text or the macrostructure, which, when combined with the microstructure, will help students create a situation model. The situation model is the complex combination of the ideas represented in the textbase and the ideas created within the student's network of world and experiential background knowledge.

Finally, Mrs. Williams will teach additional lessons using the *Autumn* informational text so as to complete the integration. The integration process requires that readers integrate the contents from the situation model held in working memory into their world knowledge network stored in long-term memory. What this means is that effortful linking of known world knowledge about the season fall or autumn (stored in long-term memory) with new knowledge about autumn from the *Autumn* text (held in working memory) is necessary for younger, less fluent readers—and even some more accomplished readers—to transfer the contents of a situation model into their world knowledge network stored in long-term memory. See Table 4.2 for lesson suggestions that correlate with each stage of Kintsch's Construction–Integration Model of Text Comprehension. All of these suggestions use multiple close readings of the book *Autumn* to support and reinforce student comprehension (the bolded lesson is Sample Lesson 1).

Table 4.2. Lesson Suggestions Using the Text *Autumn*

Autumn (Berger & Berger, 2004)

Reading Anchor Standards 1-9 for Informational Text - Kindergarten

		Key Ideas and Details
Microstructure	Standard 1	With prompting and support, ask and answer questions about key details in text. *Teaching Suggestion:* Demonstrate for students how to ask questions about the topic in the text. Encourage students to answer questions as well as asking questions of their own.
	Standard 2	**With prompting and support, identify the main topic and retell key details.** *Teaching Suggestion:* Use Sample Lesson 1.
	Standard 3	With prompting and support, describe the connection between two ideas. *Teaching Suggestion:* Discuss with students the connection between the concept of days getting shorter and cooler. How are these two ideas related? Other connections: the wind blowing and the leaves falling down; plants grow big and farmers pick the plants.
		Craft and Structure
Macrostructure	Standard 4	With prompting and support, ask and answer questions about unknown words in text. *Teaching Suggestion:* Have discussions and ask and answer questions about the following words in text: autumn, ripe, pick, store, gather, cocoons, south, fall.
	Standard 5	Identify the front cover, back cover, and title page of a book. *Teaching Suggestion:* Describe what is found on the front cover (title, picture, publisher), back cover (information about book, author, publisher), and title page (title, picture, authors, publisher location) of *Autumn*.
	Standard 6	Name the author/illustrator and define roles. *Teaching Suggestion:* Identify the author names and discuss how photographs were used instead of illustrations. Locate photo credits on copyright page.

A Focus on the Macrostructure, Text Complexity, and Range

Mr. Jensen has selected the book *Measuring Tools* (Daronco & Presti, 2011) to use in a comprehension lesson for a group of his 2nd-grade students. Mr. Jensen used the four criteria noted earlier to select a text at the appropriate level of complexity and within the appropriate range. First, Mr. Jensen selected a text of great interest to his students. Learning about

Table 4.2, *continued*

		Integration of Knowledge and Ideas
Integration	Standard 7	With prompting and support, describe relationship between photographs/text. *Teaching Suggestion:* Discuss with students how the photographs on each page align with the text. Read one page of the book and have students illustrate what they picture. Compare their picture with the photo in the book. Discuss how the photograph helps the reader picture what is going on in the text.
	Standard 8	With prompting and support, identify the reasons an author shares information about concepts. *Teaching Suggestion:* As a class or small group, make a list of all the things you know about the winter season. Explain that we learn this information about seasons through our observations. The authors did the same with the book about autumn. These authors shared information they know about autumn through their own experiences and observations.
	Standard 9	With prompting and support, identify basic similarities in and differences between two texts on same topic. *Teaching Suggestion:* Use the book *Watching the Weather* by Marcia Freeman (2007) to make these comparisons between the two books. Similarities: photographs instead of illustrations used, information gathered from observations of seasons, text aligns with pictures on page. Differences: One book is about autumn only, while the other book includes all seasons; one book has table of contents, etc.

the different tools used to measure things is fascinating for students. Students have had a range of experience with using the different tools discussed in the text. This book also supports the teaching of mathematical concepts. Thus, this book topic lends itself to multiple close readings. The use of photographs, along with the real-life examples of the tools being used, further enhances student interest. Second, the Goldilocks principle was employed, meaning that Mr. Jensen selected a text with a Lexile score in the range of 130L–500L, placing this book at the 2nd-grade level and within the Lexile level stretch bandwidth suggested by the CCSS. Third, the book selected is from the informational text genre. It lends itself well to teaching measurement concepts and it aligns with the comprehension standards for teaching informational text. Finally, the qualitative aspects provided in this particular text include photographs, a descriptive text structure, bolded text, a title that indicates the text structure, a table of contents, headings, and a glossary.

Selecting Standards and Strategies for Constructing Macrostructure and Textbase

Mr. Jensen selected the informational text *Measuring Tools* for the purpose of helping these young children develop reading comprehension skills as outlined in the CCSS and listed under the Anchor Standard cluster 2—craft and structure—for informational text. Mr. Jensen's lesson centers on Standard 5: Know and use various text features (e.g., headings, tables of contents, glossaries, electronic menus, icons) to locate key facts or information in a text. He selects two comprehension strategies to support this standard: using text features to locate information and to summarize information presented in the text.

In reading the book *Measuring Tools*, the students are being exposed to a lot of information about the many different tools used to measure objects. Making students aware of how authors organize information in text can help reveal to students the overall structure, which in turn can strengthen student comprehension. Mr. Jensen points out that this informational text is broken up into different sections, making it easier for the reader to locate information. Being able to find information quickly and easily becomes more important as students begin to read longer and more complicated texts. Mr. Jensen calls students' attention to the table of contents at the beginning of the book. He briefly reviews the types of information that students can anticipate reading based on what is shared in the table of contents. With this information provided by Mr. Jensen, the students are enabled to construct a coherent mental model or an overall picture of *Measuring Tools* at a global level, called a macrostructure. This will enable students to recognize hierarchical relationships among various key ideas in the text as they follow the organizational pattern provided in the table of contents. Authors employ a variety of text features to support the reader, and Standard 5 under Anchor Standard cluster 2 provides an opportunity for the teacher to focus on and teach students about each of these text features used by authors to organize information. Attending to the different types of text features supports students in building an overall global structure or macrostructure. Without text features, readers are left to impose their own structure and may miss key ideas and details.

Figure 4.2. Lesson 2—Supporting Construction of Macrostructure to Complete Text-base

CCSS Anchor Standard: Craft and Structure #5 (2nd Grade)—Know and use various text features to locate key facts or information in a text.
Materials: Copies of *Measuring Tools* (Daronco & Presti, 2011) for teacher and each student, chart paper, marker.

Lesson Objective/Explanation: (Teacher wording is in italics.) *Today we will be learning how authors organize information so we can find and read it more easily. Learning to identify how books are organized can help you remember and understand the information the author is trying to tell you.*

Teacher Modeling: (Teacher takes a picture walk through the book *Measuring Tools* and models for students how to "think aloud" about the contents of information shared on the page.) *On this page, I can see the author is telling me about the tools people use to measure how long something is.* (Teacher highlights the fact that all the information on pages 4–7 is about the different ways to measure length.) *I'm going to write the word "length" on my chart and summarize the information I learned about measuring length. Oh look, now on the next two pages there is information about the tools people use to measure weight or how heavy something is. Before I read on, I am going to picture in my mind the different types of tools that I have used before that measure how heavy something is.* (Teacher checks to verify that these tools are included and there are no new tools he didn't think of.) *I'm going to write the word weight on my chart below the word "length." Next, I'll record what I learned about measuring weight.* (Teacher explains to students that he notices there are pieces of information organized on each page and that the author has done something to help the reader keep track of all of this information. Teacher turns to the first page of the book and shows students the table of contents. He points out the pages about length and weight and demonstrates how to use the table of contents to find the page with the information.)

Guided Practice (Scaffolding): *Now I am ready to have you help me. Let's look at the table of contents to see what category of measurement the author going to tell us about next.* (Have a student read the next line in the table of contents.) *What is the category?* (The student reads the page that talks about the types of tools used to measure volume. Student turns to p. 10 as directed by the table of contents and summarizes the information about tools used to measure volume.) (Teacher has the students summarize what they read. Teacher records the word "volume" and the student summary. Teacher invites another student to read the next line of the table of contents and directs students to locate the page that explains the tools used to measure temperature. Teacher records the word "temperature" on the chart and the student summary of information.) *Can you see how the author is organizing the information so it is easy for the reader to find?*

Independent Practice (Gradual Release): *You are now ready to try this on your own.* (Teacher instructs the students to use the table of contents to locate the page about the tools used to measure time. Teacher has students summarize what they have read and record the information on the chart.)

Figure 4.2. Lesson 2, *continued*

Assessment: Teacher explains to the students that together they have read the book and learned how to use a table of contents. This text feature helps the reader find information quickly. Teacher has students compare the table of contents with the information recorded on the chart. Does the information students gathered reflect the contents of the book? If time permits, teacher has students use additional books that contain a table of contents to locate information in the text and summarize the information on a piece of paper.

The following lesson (see Figure 4.2) was designed by Mr. Jensen to assist students in constructing a macrostructure of this particular informational text. Explicit instruction provides a great way to model, scaffold, and support the construction of the macrostructure (text understandings drawn from text features, structure, and literary devices). Researchers encourage the use of explicit instruction, modeling, and discussion to teach text structure and text features utilized in informational texts that may go unnoticed by students (Cunningham & Allington, 1999; Pearson & Duke, 2002; Pearson & Fielding, 1991; Williams, Hall, & Lauer, 2004).

At this point, the lesson designed to build the macrostructure of the *Measuring Tools* informational text is complete, but Mr. Jensen will still have work to do and lessons to teach that will continue to support students in building a macrostructure with this text. Teaching other craft and structure standards (Standards 4–6) will require additional close readings of the text, with each lesson emphasizing a different aspect of the text. Additionally, Mr. Jensen will need to teach more lessons that will require multiple close readings of the book *Measuring Tools* with an emphasis this time on skills described in the key ideas and details standards (Standards 1–3 informational text). These additional lessons will help students to build the microstructure, which, when combined with the macrostructure, will help students create a situation model. The situation model is the complex combination of the ideas represented in the textbase and the ideas created within the student's network of world and experiential background knowledge.

Finally, Mr. Jensen will teach additional lessons using the *Measuring Tools* informational text so as to complete the integration process. The integration process requires that readers integrate the contents from the situation model held in working memory into their world knowledge network stored in long-term memory. What this means is that conscious, effortful linking of known world knowledge about the tools used to measure things (stored in long-term memory) with new knowledge about measurement from the *Measuring Tools* text (held in working memory) is necessary for younger, less fluent readers—and even some more accomplished readers—to transfer the contents of a situation model into their world knowledge network stored in long-term memory. See Table 4.3 for lesson suggestions that correlate with each stage of Kintsch's Construction–Integration Model of Text Comprehension. All of these lesson suggestions use multiple close readings of the book *Measuring Tools* to support and reinforce student comprehension (the bolded lesson is Sample Lesson 2).

INTEGRATING TEXT KNOWLEDGE WITH BACKGROUND KNOWLEDGE

Text Complexity and Range

Ms. Rodriguez has selected the book *From Seed to Dandelion* (Weiss, 2008) to use in a comprehension lesson for a group of her 3rd-grade students. Ms. Rodriguez used the four criteria noted above to select a text at the appropriate level of complexity and within the appropriate range. First, Ms. Rodriguez selected a text of great interest to her students. Learning about how a dandelion puff soars through the air and lands on the ground to become a dandelion is intriguing to students. Students have had a range of experiences with seeds and plants, and will bring this background knowledge to the text and use new information presented to build the microstructure. The sequence text structure provides the overall organization for the information in this book, which helps students to build the macrostructure. Additionally, the text aligns with concepts being taught in 3rd grade. Thus, this book topic lends itself to multiple close readings. Second, the Goldilocks principle was employed, meaning the text selected by Ms. Rodriguez has a Lexile score of 600L, which is in the range of 330L–700L placing this book within the Lexile level stretch bandwidth suggested by the CCSS. Third, the book selected is from the informational text genre. It can be used to teach the life cycle of a plant. Finally, the qualitative aspects provided in this particular text include photographs, a sequence text structure, bolded text, call-outs, a title that indicates text structure, a table of contents, headings, and an index.

Table 4.3. Lesson Suggestions Using the Text *Measuring Tools*

Measuring Tools (Daronco & Presti, 2011)

Reading Anchor Standards 1-9 for Informational Text - 2nd Grade

		Key Ideas and Details
Microstructure	Standard 1	Ask and answer questions about key details in text. *Teaching Suggestion:* Spend time asking and answering questions with students after reading text. Some questions to consider: What are some things we measure? What does a ruler measure? How are a clock and a watch the same/different?
	Standard 2	Identify the main topic and retell key details. *Teaching Suggestion:* Use the title to determine main topic. Use each page to identify key details: length, weight, volume, temperature, and time.
	Standard 3	Describe the connection between two ideas or pieces of information. *Teaching Suggestion:* Both the tape measure and ruler are used to measure length. How are they alike/different? Do the same for the outdoor thermometer/oral thermometer, and the watch/clock. How do these tools measure the same thing? How do these tools measure different things?
		Craft and Structure
Macrostructure	Standard 4	Ask and answer questions to help determine or clarify the meaning of words and phrases. *Teaching Suggestion:* Have discussions and ask and answer questions about the following words or phrases in text: measure, in half, temperature, length, lumbar, scale, volume, weight. Also, see the Glossary at the end.
	Standard 5	**Know and use the various text features to locate key facts and information.** *Teaching Suggestion:* Use Sample Lesson 2.
	Standard 6	Distinguish between information provided in pictures and those provided in text. *Teaching Suggestion:* Do a picture walk with students and go through the book, discussing with students the information that is shared through the photographs. Discuss how text enhances our understanding and provides information about the topic. Discuss how photos reinforce the information the author is trying to share.

Table 4.3, *continued*

		Integration of Knowledge and Ideas
Integration	Standard 7	Use the illustrations and details in a text to describe key ideas.
		Teaching Suggestion: Do another close reading of the text, asking students to pay attention this time to the photographs. Ask students to examine the photographs provided and discuss how these share additional information with the reader.
	Standard 8	Identify the reasons an author gives to support points in a text.
		Teaching Suggestion: Read pp. 6–7 with students and discuss how the man is measuring something long and so the ruler won't work. Why won't the ruler work (pp. 4–5)? What is the author trying to share about when to use a grocery scale/bathroom scale (pp. 8–9)? What reasons does the author use to support this idea?
	Standard 9	Identify basic similarities in and differences between two texts on the same topic.
		Teaching Suggestion: Use the book *Using Tools* by Brenda Parkes (1998) to make these comparisons between the two books.
		Similarities: Photographs instead of illustrations used, both books discuss the types of tools we use, both books demonstrate how tools are used.
		Differences: Different tools are introduced in these two books; the second book talks more about how tools are used to fix things, while the first book is about using tools to measure things.

Selecting Standards and Comprehension Strategies

Ms. Rodriguez selected the informational text *From Seed to Dandelion* for the purpose of helping her students develop reading comprehension skills as outlined in the CCSS and listed under Anchor Standard cluster 3—integration of knowledge and ideas—for informational text. Ms. Rodriguez's lesson centers on Standard 7: Use information gained from illustrations (e.g., maps, photographs) and other words in a text to demonstrate understanding of the text (e.g., where, when, why, and how key events occur). She selects the discussion comprehension strategy to support this standard.

In reading the book *From Seed to Dandelion*, the students are being exposed to a lot of information about the process of a seed becoming a plant. The integration process, as described in the CI Model of Text Comprehension (Kintsch, 2013), requires that readers integrate the contents of the situation model held in working memory into their world knowledge network stored in their long-term memory. Prior to this integration lesson, Ms. Rodriguez will need to teach lessons that help create a microstructure and macrostructure so the textbase and the situation model can be formed. Once these have been established, the students are ready for Ms. Rodriguez's integration lesson. So as to avoid what Kintsch (2013) calls *encapsulated knowledge*, Ms. Rodriguez will need to assist her students in integrating the contents of their situation models into the contents of their global or world knowledge. Otherwise, their encapsulated knowledge will remain linked to a single text or situation model, and isolated from the contents of the reader's world knowledge network.

The following lesson was designed by Ms. Rodriguez to assist students in integrating the microstructure and macrostructure of the text and creating a situation model. Explicit instruction provides a great way to model, scaffold, and support students in integrating the wide range of information they have gathered. Researchers encourage the use of explicit instruction, modeling, and discussion to teach different text features and aspects of informational texts (Cunningham & Allington, 1999; Pearson & Duke, 2002; Pearson & Fielding, 1991; Williams et al., 2004).

This particular lesson (see Figure 4.3), designed to help students integrate knowledge from the book *From Seed to Dandelion*, is now complete, but Ms. Rodriguez will still have work to do and lessons to teach that will continue to support students in building knowledge, as outlined in Kintsch's Construction–Integration Model of Text Comprehension. First, Ms. Rodriguez will need to teach lessons that will require multiple close readings of the book *From Seed to Dandelion*, with an emphasis on the key ideas and details standards (Standards 1–3 of the CCSS for the comprehension of informational text). These lessons will help students to build the microstructure.

Next, Ms. Rodriguez will need to teach the lessons using craft and structure standards (Standards 4–6). This will require additional close readings of *From Seed to Dandelion*, with each lesson emphasizing a different aspect of the text features and structures.

Finally, Ms. Rodriguez will teach additional lessons using the *From Seed to Dandelion* informational text so as to complete the integration process. The integration process requires that readers integrate the

Figure 4.3. Lesson 3—Supporting Integration to Create a Situation Model

CCSS Anchor Standard: Integration of Knowledge and Ideas #7 (3rd Grade)—Use information gained from illustrations (e.g., maps, photographs) and other words in a text to demonstrate understanding of the text (e.g., where, when, why, and how key events occur).

Materials: One copy of *From Seed to Dandelion* (Weiss, 2008), white paper, markers or crayons, Post-it notes to cover photographs in book.

Lesson Objective/Explanation: (Teacher wording in italics.) *Today we will be learning how use photographs and illustrations shared by the author to learn information presented in a book. Learning how to use photos and illustrations can help you remember and understand the information the author is trying to tell you.*

Teacher Modeling: (Hold up the book *From Seed to Dandelion* and discuss with students what the text might be about. Encourage students to use the clues from the title as well as the picture on the front cover. Be sure to point out the three smaller inset pictures as well. Explain to students that the author of this book used photographs to share additional information or to explain the information presented in the text. Read page 8 to students. Cover up the picture with a Post-it note.) The text on this page describes what a dandelion flower looks like. *Hmmm. I wonder what a floret looks like.* Using the poster paper, draw a picture of a flower and discuss with students what you think a floret looks like. Explain why you think a floret looks the way you drew it. Draw a typical flower. Now show students the picture you drew and ask if it is the same as the photograph of the floret. Explain to students that what we typically think a flower looks like is not necessarily how a floret looks. *It's a good thing the author shared a picture so we can see exactly what a floret looks like. Photos and illustrations help us understand new concepts and ideas. We might have some ideas based on our past experiences or based on books and pictures of flowers, but in this case, a floret doesn't look the same as other flowers we have seen.* Discuss with students the importance of the photograph in aiding the reader's comprehension of the text.

Guided Practice (Scaffolding): *Now let's have you join me. Let's read the next page. I have covered up the photographs. Let's read and then draw a picture of what we think the author is talking about.* Have students (or the teacher) read page 10. The author describes the different stages a dandelion plant goes through including the floret to the seed to the yellow flower to the stem and finally to the white fluff. Based on the information shared by the author, have students draw a picture of the dandelion seed. Next, have students share their pictures and explain how they knew what to draw. (Students will be using information from life experiences they have had with seeds and from other books they have read about seeds and what they look like.) Next, have students continue this same process using the information shared on page 12 about how the dandelion fluff flies like a parachute through the air. Be sure to have rich discussions about student illustrations compared with the author's photographs and about how these images help students integrate information and strengthen comprehension.

Figure 4.3, *continued*

Independent Practice (Gradual Release): *You are now ready to try this on your own. Let's have you read each page and illustrate what you read about.* Instruct the students to read the information on these remaining pages of the book: Page 14 about the taproot, page 16 about the green shoot, and page 20 about the life cycle of the dandelion. Have students read the page, draw what they think the author means, remove the Post-it and compare their picture with the author's photograph, and discuss what they learn from the photograph.

Assessment: Explain to the students that together you have read the book and learned how important the photographs are in this informational text. The photographs help the reader understand more clearly the life cycle of a dandelion and they also help the student integrate background knowledge with knowledge presented in the text.

contents from the situation model held in working memory into their world knowledge network stored in long-term memory. See Table 4.4 for lesson suggestions that correlate with each stage of Kintsch's Construction–Integration Model of Text Comprehension. All of these lesson suggestions use multiple close readings of the book *From Seed to Dandelion* to support and reinforce student comprehension (the bolded lesson is Sample Lesson 3).

THE BENEFITS OF USING THE CI MODEL AND STANDARDS TO TEACH INFORMATIONAL TEXT COMPREHENSION

The use of informational text for teaching reading comprehension is mandated in the CCSS for teaching reading in the primary grades. The Construction–Integration Model of Comprehension necessitates the reading and rereading of informational texts for targeted, specific purposes. Students analyze texts from a variety of perspectives to create a microstructure, macrostructure, and situation model. Students examine the phrases, sentences, text structure, visual and graphical devices, and other unique informational text features, for example, glossary, indexes, and so on. Informational texts open up a window of world knowledge for primary-grade students to gain knowledge about the world around them.

Table 4.4. Lesson Suggestions Using the Text *From Seed to Dandelion*

From Seed to Dandelion (Weiss, 2008)

Reading Anchor Standards 1-9 for Informational Text - 3rd Grade

		Key Ideas and Details
Microstructure	Standard 1	Ask and answer questions to demonstrate understanding of text, referring explicitly to the text as basis for answers. *Teaching Suggestion:* Model for students how to ask and answer questions by quoting explicitly from the text. Example: What is a floret? "Each tiny flower is called a floret" (p. 8). Have students take turns asking and answering questions.
	Standard 2	Determine the main idea of the text; recount key details and how they support main ideas. *Teaching Suggestion:* Demonstrate how the title helps the reader understand the main idea of text. Read book and then close book and ask students to recount from memory the key ideas. What helped them remember the key details? How do these details support the main idea?
	Standard 3	Describe the relationship between a series of scientific ideas or concepts . . . using language that pertains to time and sequence. *Teaching Suggestion:* Have students create a visual that outlines the steps of how a seed turns into a dandelion. Encourage students to use cue words such as first, second, then, etc.
		Craft and Structure
Macrostructure	Standard 4	Determine the meaning of general academic specific words or phrases in text related to grade 3 topic or subject areas. *Teaching Suggestion:* Grade 3 science objectives include "describe common plants found in local environment," so have students articulate the characteristics that are unique to the dandelion plant. Words to discuss include: floret, fluff, petals, shoot, taproot, soil, blooms.
	Standard 5	Use text features to locate information in text. *Teaching Suggestion:* Use table of contents to locate information quickly (see pp. 16–17). Call out topic and have students locate page numbers and locate information on that topic.
	Standard 6	Distinguish their own point of view from that of authors. *Teaching Suggestion:* Have students list their opinions related to dandelions. What do they think of dandelions? What do they know others think of dandelions? Then have students make a list of the points of view the author shares. (Example: The author finds them interesting and describes the life cycle in poetic ways . . . like tiny parachutes.)

Table 4.4, *continued*

		Integration of Knowledge and Ideas
Integration	Standard 7	**Use information gained from illustrations and text to demonstrate understanding.** *Teaching Suggestion:* Use Sample Lesson 3.
	Standard 8	Describe the logical connection between sentences and paragraphs. *Teaching Suggestion:* Point out the sequence cue words to help show connection between sentences on pp. 15 and 16. The author uses "first" on p. 15 and "then" on p. 16.
	Standard 9	Compare and contrast most important points and key details presented in two texts on the same topic. *Teaching Suggestion:* Use the book *The Dandelion Seed's Big Dream* by Joseph Anthony (2014) to make these comparisons between the two books. Similarities: Both authors make the seed traveling seem poetic; both discuss how easily the dandelion grows. Differences: The second author draws similarities between the reader and the dandelion. The first author does not do this but rather provides a scientific discussion about the life cycle of the dandelion.

CHAPTER 5

Comprehension Assessment

CHAPTER OVERVIEW

A major complaint often heard among educators is that testing is driving instruction (Dennis, 2009). This complaint is usually an oblique reference to a sense shared among educators and even parents that too much testing occurs in schools. In the case of reading comprehension, the way in which it has been assessed in the nation's schools has strongly reflected, for all intents and purposes, how it is taught in classrooms. Reading comprehension has been defined in a variety of ways over the years, which in turn has driven changes in both comprehension instruction and assessment in classrooms.

Defining Reading Comprehension

Hundreds of years ago during early colonial times, reading, including comprehension, was defined as memory for text (Smith, 2002). If one could read well orally, provide a fluent oral rendition of a text that was marked by skillful elocution, one was considered a competent reader. However, the mark of the superlative reader went well beyond a fluent oral rendition of a text to include skillful recitation of a memorized text. This definition of reading comprehension, however, is quite problematic. With this definition of reading comprehension, it was quite possible to memorize a text, recite it skillfully, but still not understand it.

With the passage of time, reading comprehension was redefined. In 1917, Edward Thorndike reconceptualized reading comprehension as thinking or reasoning with text. This marked the beginning of an era when reading comprehension was defined as understanding text. In consequence of this definition, scholars began a search for fundamental or underlying factors that permitted readers to understand text. Davis (1944) found nine basic skills that enabled readers to understand a text:

1. Knowledge of word meanings
2. Ability to select the correct word meaning in light of its context
3. Ability to follow the organization of a passage
4. Ability to answer questions in which the answers are found explicitly in the text
5. Ability to answer questions that are in the text but not explicitly stated
6. Ability to draw inferences from a text
7. Ability to select the main idea of a text
8. Ability to recognize the use of literary devices in text to determine mood and tone
9. Ability to determine a writer's purpose, intent, or point of view

An unintended consequence stemming from the identification of these nine enabling reading comprehension skills was that reading comprehension assessment began to focus on measuring readers' abilities to perform each of these nine skilled reading behaviors in isolation. In addition, students' vocabulary knowledge and the ability to answer a variety of different levels of comprehension questions, for example, Bloom's Taxonomy, were used as *prima facie* evidence of text comprehension.

In more recent years, the definition of reading comprehension once again has undergone a change. It now is not enough to understand a text. Rather, reading comprehension currently is seen as a catalyst for connecting past knowledge and experience to information presented in a text to acquire new knowledge. Duke et al. (2011) described something called the *virtuous comprehension cycle,* virtuous used here to represent a successful and productive sequence of comprehension processes. In the virtuous comprehension cycle, past knowledge and experience beget text comprehension and then text comprehension begets the acquisition of new knowledge. The consequence of this most recent definition of reading comprehension is that reading comprehension assessment examines the additional knowledge students acquire from reading a text. Consequently, *informational text* has received particular attention due to this more recent definition of reading comprehension (Duke, 2000; NGA Center & CCSSO, 2010).

Comprehension Assessment Tasks

In practical terms, for many years now, reading comprehension has been assessed using a mere handful of assessment tasks (Dougherty-Stahl,

2009). First among these assessment tasks has been what psychologists have called a "free recall" of the text. In a free recall task, the reader is asked to retell what he/she remembers from reading the text in as complete or detailed a fashion as possible.

Second among this handful of assessment tasks has been what psychologists have called a "probed recall" of text (Dougherty-Stahl, 2009). In a probed recall task, the reader is asked questions about the text as a probe for elements remembered from reading the text but not offered up spontaneously in a free recall or retelling of a text. Consequently, students are asked to answer a series of reading comprehension questions, often at different levels of comprehension, to probe their recollection of text content.

A third reading comprehension assessment task, seldom used over the years, is the sentence verification task (Dougherty-Stahl, 2009). In the sentence verification task, students are shown a sentence and are asked to verify whether this sentence was in the text or not. It was thought that if students had read the text carefully, they'd then be more likely to recall reading a particular sentence in the text.

Comprehension: A Unitary Construct?

Another challenging aspect of reading comprehension assessment has focused on whether reading comprehension is a unitary construct (Duke, 2005). By definition, a psychological or educational construct is thought of as something constructed in and by the mind. Reading comprehension is a prime example since what is comprehended from a text is constructed totally in and by the mind. At a practical level, comprehension assessment often has been treated as a unitary construct. Students have been asked in the past to evidence their comprehension through performance of a singular, traditional task—answering probing questions after reading a text. More recently, literacy scholars have called into question the idea that reading comprehension is a unitary construct, arguing that there are multiple ways to demonstrate comprehension of a text (Duke, 2005).

For example, if students are asked to retell a text, this is not the same kind of assessment task as answering probing questions about a text. Similarly, if students are asked to summarize a text orally or in writing, this is not the same task as retelling a text. When retelling, students strive to reproduce the text as completely as possible, including top-level structure, most important ideas, and supporting details. When writing or telling a summary of a text, only the top-level structure and the most important ideas are retold or written. In essence, the fact that multiple tasks can be used to demonstrate comprehension is strong evidence that comprehension is a multifaceted, nonunitary construct that can be demonstrated through completion of a variety of tasks. As Kintsch and Kintsch (2005) succinctly stated, "There is no uniform comprehension process to be measured" (p. 84). Or as Nell Duke (2005) phrased it when speaking of comprehension assessment, "Comprehension of what; for what?" (p. 97).

Two Major Types of Comprehension Assessments

Comprehension assessment, like many other types of educational and literacy assessments, can be of two different types:

1. *Summative* or what some educators call standardized and sometimes high-stakes assessment
2. *Formative*, typically produced by classroom educators for measuring student responses to specific teaching events (McKenna & Stahl, 2009)

In today's Common Core classroom, summative or standardized, high-stakes tests of comprehension can be found in Smarter Balanced (www.smarterbalanced.org/practice-test/), PARCC (parcc.pearson.com/practice-tests/), Sage (sageportal.org/training-tests/), or Aspire (www.discoveractaspire.org/assessments/test-items/) testing batteries. These summative assessments rely heavily upon the completion of a singular comprehension assessment task—reading a text and answering questions. Consequently, summative, standardized reading comprehension tests continue to define reading comprehension at a practical level as answering questions about a text—especially answering text-dependent questions (Frey & Fisher, 2013).

On the other hand, classroom teachers are compelled to assist their students to meet the CCSS for reading literature and informational texts (Cummins, 2013; Lewis, Walpole, & McKenna, 2014; McLaughlin & Overturf, 2013; Shanahan, 2015). However, the CCSS do not confine the definition of reading comprehension to the performance of a single task or demonstration of comprehension—such as answering questions. Instead the CCSS require that students perform a variety of tasks, such as retelling; identifying story or text structure; recognizing different types of texts; identifying author, illustrator, perspective, and point of view; comparing and contrasting ideas, events, and characters in text; providing textual evidence for answers to questions; determining main ideas and key details; and using text features, and so on, as multiple ways of demonstrating text comprehension.

If teachers want to know whether their students can meet the CCSS Reading Standards, then formative comprehension assessment tasks will need to be designed to assess the attainment of the CCSS for reading literature and information text. That is what the remainder of this chapter will help teachers accomplish.

However, basing formative assessments solely upon the CCSS Reading Standards fails to provide a theoretical framework to guide comprehension assessment. As we have noted repeatedly throughout this book, neither comprehension instruction nor comprehension assessment can be adequately informed unless teachers are working from a clearly articulated theoretical framework of text comprehension (Kucan et al., 2011). We briefly review the CI Model of text comprehension so that it can be used by teachers to inform and guide the work of designing formative reading comprehension assessment tasks to measure whether their students are meeting the requirements of the CCSS for reading literature and informational texts.

ASSESSMENT OF CCSS READING STANDARDS
FOR COMPREHENSION

It is our collective assertion that reading comprehension assessment informed by the CI Model provides a clear guide for designing a comprehensive collection of formative reading comprehension assessment tasks. Using the CI Model of Text Comprehension to design formative, standards-based comprehension assessment tasks ensures that teachers determine how well or whether their students can process texts, literature and informational, at multiple levels of text comprehension. In Figure 5.1, we show a model of comprehension assessment that captures and organizes the multiple levels of the CI text comprehension model.

Figure 5.1 illustrates how a theoretically informed assessment of reading comprehension, based on the CI Model, addresses multiple levels of text comprehension processing. At the top of this framework, we show two levels of text comprehension processing, micro and macro levels, as found in the construction phase of the CI Model. For teachers to understand and use this CI Model–based comprehension assessment

Figure 5.1. A Comprehension Assessment Model Based on the Construction–Integration Model of Text Comprehension

CONSTRUCTION

Micro Process

- Word meaning knowledge
- Phrase and sentence meaning
- Details vs. key ideas
- Cohesion connections

Textbase

Macro Process

- Text features
- Story or text structure
- Key ideas vs. details
- Answer text dependent questions
- Literacy devices

Textbase

INTEGRATION (Textbase and Schema)

Situation Process

- Retelling/Describe
- Point of view/Perspective
- Answer inferential and schema-dependent questions

World Knowledge Acquisition

- Summarize
- Reporting/Presentation
- Ask questions
- Compare/Contrast

Low Level

High Level

framework, we provided additional illustrations, in Table 1.1, of how each of the major processes of the CI Model–based framework, construction and integration (pictured in Figure 5.1), is related to the four CCSS Anchor Standard clusters and the ten individual Anchor Standards for reading literature and informational text.

DESIGNING A FORMATIVE COMPREHENSION ASSESSMENT PLAN FOR GRADES K–2

In this section, we discuss how teachers can design a comprehensive, formative assessment plan for the primary grades using the CI Model as a guide linked to the CCSS for reading literature and informational text. To begin, teachers need to understand the order in which the multiple levels of comprehension processing represented in the CI Model are to be assessed. We say this because if students aren't able to *construct* an adequate textbase from reading a text (a lower level textbase construction process), then higher level comprehension processes involving *integration* will most likely be impeded. In Figure 5.2, we outline the order of the steps we believe are important for teachers to consider when designing formative assessment tasks for measuring student mastery of K–2 CCSS Anchor Standards for reading literature and informational text.

To help clarify how the process of designing CI Model–based and CCSS Reading Standards–based formative comprehension assessment tasks can be accomplished, we discuss and elaborate upon each step shown in Figure 5.2.

Selecting a Challenging Complex Text for Assessment

In many cases, publishers do the job of text selection for teachers—as is the case in most school- or district-adopted core reading programs. In other cases, the opportunity to select an appropriately challenging, engaging, and supportive text for designing formative comprehension assessment falls on the classroom teacher.

Shanahan et al. (2010) made five recommendations in an Institute of Education Sciences K–3 practice guide for improving reading comprehension instruction. Recommendation # 4 states that teachers "select texts purposefully to support comprehension development" (p. 30). This recommendation suggests that teachers select texts from multiple genres that contain a richness and depth of ideas and information. Teachers

Figure 5.2. CI Model of Text Comprehension

Select a Challenging Complex Text Heading:
- Consider topic or theme of text
- Lexile stretch guide level bandwidth
- Genre
- Text features, structure, author perspectives, and literary devices

CCSS Reading Standards	Assessment Task
LEVEL 1: Microlevel Process	
Anchor Standard L4, I4	Vocabulary Word Meaning
Anchor Standard L4, I4	Phrase Meanings
Anchor Standard L1, I1	Sentence Meanings
Anchor Standard I3	Cohesion Connections
Anchor Standard L1, I1	Ask and Answer Detail Questions
LEVEL 2: Macrolevel Process	
Anchor Standard L3, L7, I5, I6, I7	Story or Text Features
Anchor Standard L3, L5, I5	Story or Text Structure
Anchor Standard L2, L3, I2, I3	Key Ideas/Main Topic
Anchor Standard L1, I1, I2	Answer Text Dependent Question
Anchor Standard L5	Text Gear Recognition
LEVEL 3: Integrate Textbase and Schema	
Anchor Standard L2, L7, I2, I7	Retelling, Describing
Anchor Standard L6	Points of View, Perspective
Anchor Standard I3, I8	Inferences and Schema Dependent Questions
LEVEL 4: Integrate Situation Model Into World Knowledge Network	
Anchor Standard L2, L9, I2, I9	Summarize
Anchor Standard L2, L9, I2, I9	Reporting/Presentation
Anchor Standard NA	Ask Questions
Anchor Standard L9, I9	Compare/Contrast

select texts to assess reading comprehension where the word recognition and comprehension difficulty are appropriate for their students' reading abilities and for the instructional activity. They also select texts that support the purposes, standards, and levels of comprehension processing in the CI Model (Kintsch, 2013).

The process of selecting an appropriately challenging and complex text for reading comprehension assessment directly addresses the intent of Reading Standard cluster 4—range of reading and level of text complexity—and individual reading Anchor Standard 10. When selecting a text to support informal or formative reading comprehension assessment task development, teachers would do well to consider four important indicators:

1. The reader–text match
2. The quantitative level of difficulty of the text
3. The qualitative obstacles to comprehension at each level of text comprehension processing
4. The comprehension tasks, including dialogue and discussion, to be assessed at each level of text comprehension processing represented in the CI Model

Teachers consider the topic or theme of the text to be read for assessment and whether it is likely to be of interest to students as a part of the reader–text match. Next, teachers apply the Goldilocks principle when selecting a text for designing formative comprehension assessment tasks—a challenge level that is just right—for the grade level of the students. To do this, teachers select texts for assessment that are within the Lexile level stretch bandwidth suggested by the CCSS (see www.lexile. com/using-lexile/lexile-measures-and-the-ccssi/text-complexity-grade-bands-and-lexile-ranges/).

After this, teachers consider the genre of the text to be selected for reading comprehension assessment. To maintain the CCSS suggested proportion of 50/50 literature to informational text reading, teachers alternate selecting literature and informational texts when designing formative comprehension assessment tasks.

Teachers need to pre-read the selected texts to determine qualitative aspects of the text difficulty that may prove challenging to students. Qualitative aspects of the text that make comprehension difficult are almost always related to what the author chooses to include in or exclude from the text. For example, authors may fail to include connecting and signal words, headings, illustrations, photos, or a glossary. Authors may write using a clearly identifiable text structure or employ mixed or multiple text structures within a single text. Other elements of text that present difficulties for students include shifts in perspective or one's point of view, or the use of multiple timelines or multiple story plots.

Designing Formative Comprehension Assessment Tasks

Formative reading comprehension assessment based on the CI Model of Text Comprehension and the CCSS anchor reading standards for literature and informational texts requires that readers engage in multiple levels of text processing to successfully demonstrate text comprehension. For example, it is entirely possible that some students who are able to locate answers to text-dependent questions at the sentence level, cannot answer text-dependent questions that require making connections across sentences. Successful text comprehension begins with the *construction* of a textbase (micro and macro processes) and then proceeds to creating a situation model, or an interpretation of what the text means. *Integration* processes require students to engage in strategies to integrate the situation model of text into students' long-term store of background knowledge and life experience. The four CCSS reading standard clusters and ten individual Reading Anchor Standards are arranged into a process-driven sequence that follows the multiple levels of comprehension processing in the CI Model of Text Comprehension beginning with key ideas and details, progressing to author's craft and structure, and then onto integrating knowledge and ideas so as to assess comprehension processes at multiple and higher levels of meaning.

In practice, this means that the design of formative comprehension assessment tasks informed by the CI Model begins with assessing those CCSS Reading Anchor Standards that are at the lowest levels of text comprehension processing and then proceeding in a systematic fashion to assess those that are at deeper or higher levels of text processing.

Rather than selecting a single Reading Standard to assess text comprehension, as has been common practice in the past, teachers who possess theoretical knowledge of the CI Model select individual Reading Anchor Standards that are sequenced from lower to higher levels of text processing, as found in the CI Model. In Table 1.1, we have linked individual Reading Anchor Standards in a sequence of text-processing levels from lower level construction tasks to higher level integration tasks as described by the CI Model's multiple levels of text processing.

For example, teachers begin designing formative comprehension assessment tasks by selecting an individual Reading Anchor Standard(s) that relates to the CI Model's construction phase of text processing—micro-level processing. An example of such a standard is Reading Anchor Standard 1, shown below.

1. Ask and answer questions about key details in a text.

Next, proceeding from the lowest levels of construction comprehension processes (micro processes) to higher level text comprehension processes, teachers might select Reading Anchor Standard 5 to assess the next level of text processing—macro text processing.

5. Know and use various text features (e.g., headings, tables of contents, glossaries, electronic menus, icons) to locate key facts or information in a text.

Finally, teachers assess their students' integration of knowledge and ideas to create a situation model as described in the CI Model of text comprehension by selecting a Reading Anchor Standard such as Standard 9.

9. Compare and contrast the most important points presented by two texts on the same topic.

Standard 9 requires students to compare and contrast key ideas presented in two texts on the same topic. At this level of text processing, where teachers assess whether students can create a situation model of the text and then integrate the contents of the situation model into their world knowledge network, students are asked to compare and contrast text-based information coupled with their own background knowledge.

FORMATIVE ASSESSMENT TASKS THAT LINK CI TEXT-PROCESSING LEVELS AND ANCHOR STANDARDS

To illustrate the process of designing formative comprehension assessment tasks for measuring students' proficiency with the CCSS for reading literature and information text, we begin by selecting a 2nd-grade text.

Step 1: Selecting a Text for Designing Formative Comprehension Assessment Tasks

First, we determine a topic or theme in which children have an interest so that they will sustain attention on the text during assessment. The book we have selected is titled *From Cocoa Bean to Chocolate* by Robin Nelson

(2003). It is hard to imagine a 2nd-grade student who doesn't enjoy eating chocolate! Next, we determine whether this title is an appropriately challenging and complex text for 2nd grade. We go to the Lexile.com website and search for text complexity grade bands and associated Lexile bands. We find as we consult this website that grades 2–3 span Lexile scores from 420L–820L. Next, we enter the title of the text we have chosen on the Lexile.com website and search for the title. We find that this particular text has a Lexile of 550L which is within the 2nd-grade level bandwidth of 420l–620L. We also make sure that we have selected alternate genres to maintain the 50/50 proportion of literature and informational texts. In this case, we've selected an informational text.

After this, we pre-read the text in preparation for designing our formative comprehension assessment tasks. After reading, we find this is an excellent, even exemplary text that employs a single text structure, a *sequential* or *procedural* text structure. The author also provides readers with additional text features such as a table of contents, bolded vocabulary words that are found in a glossary, and an index. There are copious photos of the process of making chocolate from cocoa beans. One element missing in this text, with the exception of the word *then*, is the use of sequential signal words, such as *first, second, third*, or *to begin, next, after*, and so on. Students who read this text will need to infer or impose the use of these cohesion connector or signal terms to render their comprehension of the text coherent.

Step 2: Constructing Micro-Processing-Level Comprehension Assessment Tasks

The CI Model begins with *micro* processing, the lowest level of text comprehension processing, to construct a textbase. Micro processing focuses attention on constructing meaning from words, phrases, and sentences using cohesion connections or signal terms to construct meaning across sentences. Using the CI Model as a guide, as shown in Figure 5.2, we connect this level of comprehension processing, micro processing, to specific CCSS Reading Anchor Standards for informational texts. As we consult the information in Figure 5.2, we see that several assessment tasks could be designed at the micro–text–processing level. For use in this particular illustration, we selected Reading Anchor Standard 1 for Informational Text: Ask and answer questions about key details in a text. To design this part of our formative assessment of students' text comprehension, we confine our questions to one of the micro text elements noted previously—word meanings, phrase and sentence meanings, or cohesion connections, or a combination of them. In this example, we ask students to answer a series of *maze* assessment questions. A maze question can be designed by selecting a sentence from the text and replacing a single word in the sentence with a stack or series of words shown within parentheses. Maze questions typically are thought to assess sentence-level comprehension, but also may assess word-meaning knowledge. Teachers need to construct a sufficient number of maze questions, usually seven or more, so that a student's failure to correctly answer only one or two questions would not lead to erroneous conclusions that the student isn't comprehending text at the word, phrase, or sentence levels. Maze tasks are useful to assess whether students can answer questions about *key details* in text, as is expected in CCSS Reading Anchor Standard 1 for Informational Text.

Figure 5.3 presents several examples of maze tasks from the text *From Cocoa Beans to Chocolate* (Nelson, 2003).

After students have had the chance to read the entire assessment text *From Cocoa Bean to Chocolate* (Nelson, 2003), they are asked to circle or mark the correct word that makes sense in each maze task by using information from the sentence, their background knowledge, and the text they have read. Students are allowed to look back at the text if needed. For students to score satisfactorily on this task, they should receive a score of 80% or higher. Teachers should note the types of errors students make on maze items to determine what types of problems, if any, they may be having at the micro–text–processing level.

There are other types of formative assessment tasks that could be constructed for the micro level of comprehension processing (see Figure 5.2). We can design a cohesion connection assessment task at the micro–text–processing level, once again using a maze task. For example, using the same title, *From Cocoa Beans to Chocolate* (Nelson, 2003), we created the following maze assessment tasks for different levels of micro text processing, including word meanings, phrase meaning, and making cohesion connections using signal or cohesion terms (see Figure 5.4).

In addition to maze tasks for assessing CCSS Reading Standards at the construction/micro-processing level, teachers might consider the following additional options: (1) paraphrasing, (2) vertical structuring, and (3) graphic organizers.

In *paraphrase assessment* tasks, students are instructed to read a phrase or sentence similar to the one that follows: It is easier to take the shells off beans that have been roasted. The students are instructed: Do not

Figure 5.3: Maze Questions Focused on Key Details in Text

Maze Example Set 1:

    Cocoa beans grow on cocoa (bushes, trees, flowers).
bushes

    Cocoa beans grow on cocoa trees.
flowers

Maze Example Set 2:

    Cocoa beans are taken out of the (seeds, trees, pods) to dry in the sun for many days.
seeds

    Cocoa beans are taken out of the trees to dry in the sun for many days.
pods

Maze Example Set 3:

    Mashing the beans turns them into a soft paste called (cocoa butter, chocolate, chocolate syrup).
cocoa butter

    Mashing the beans turns them into a soft paste called chocolate powder.
chocolate syrup

Figure 5.4: Different Types of Formative Comprehension Tasks at the Micro–Text-Processing Level of the CI Model

Example for Word Meanings:

    A factory is a place where things are (shipped, stored, made).
shipped

    A factory is a place where things are stored.
made

Example for Phrases:

    Cocoa beans are taken out of the (seeds, trees, pods)
seeds

    Cocoa beans are taken out of the trees
pods

Example for Cohesion Connections:

    Workers cut the pods from the trees. (Next, Before, First) the workers open the pods with a large knife.
Before

    Workers cut the pods from the trees. Next, the workers open the pods with a large knife.
First

repeat the sentence; think about it and tell me what it says using your own words. Teachers score the paraphrase as correct when students use their own words and capture the correct meaning of the sentence. Paraphrasing can be a quick check during text discussions to assess students' comprehension of phrases and sentences.

Vertical structuring assessment, much like sentence combining, is an excellent formative assessment task to use when evaluating students' use of cohesion connections that signal relationships among several key details within or across sentences (Gillam & Reutzel, 2013). For example, a teacher might list the following sentences in an assessment task:

> The beans are cleaned in the chocolate factory.
> The beans are roasted in the chocolate factory.

Students are asked to (a) make these two sentences into one sentence through inserting specific words in a single sentence and deleting repeated words:

> The beans are cleaned and roasted in the chocolate factory.

or (b) sequence these sentences using cohesion connection words, in this case sequential connections:

> The beans are *first* cleaned in the chocolate factory, *then* they are roasted.

When students demonstrate the ability to manipulate language through paraphrasing and vertical structuring, teachers are well assured they can attend to, understand, and think about key details in the text in order to eventually grow their knowledge.

Finally, the use of *graphic organizer assessments* at the construction/micro-processing level of the CI Model provides yet another alternative task for assessing students' abilities to attend to and comprehend key details in text. Here again, graphic organizer tasks can be designed to probe micro–text–processing abilities at the word, phrase, or sentence levels, or the ability to use local cohesion connections to understand key ideas among or across sentences. Using our same text, *From Cocoa Beans to Chocolate* (Nelson, 2003), we illustrate several graphic organizer "fill in the missing elements" tasks for assessing each of several micro-processing levels (see Figure 5.5).

Figure 5.5. Graphic Organizer Assessment Tasks

Example for Word Meanings:

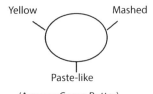

(Answer: Cocoa Butter)

Example for Phrases

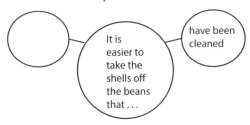

(Answer: Have been roasted)

Example for Sentences

Order: Number from 1-3

(Answer: 3, 1, 2)

Example for Cohesion Connections

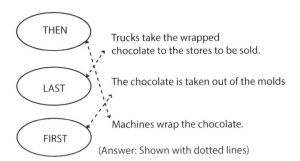

(Answer: Shown with dotted lines)

Although we have provided examples of assessing the CI Model's construction/micro-processing level and linking these examples to CCSS Reading Standards using information texts, these same types of formative assessment tasks can be used to create literature (narrative prose and poetry) assessment tasks as well.

Step 3: Constructing Macro–Processing–Level Assessment Tasks

Next in the multiple levels of the CI Model progressing from low to high levels of comprehension, we designed formative macro-level comprehension assessment tasks to uncover student understanding of the features, words, and phrases found in text that signal how texts are organized, including glossaries, headings, graphics, photos, tables of contents, figures, indexes in informational texts and foreshadowing and flashbacks in narrative texts, and linked to Reading Anchor Standards for informational text, as shown in Figure 5.2. As we examine the guidance provided in Figure 5.2, we note that we could ask students to perform several formative comprehension assessment tasks to indicate their comprehension at the macro–text–processing level. These tasks might focus on students' knowledge or use of text structure and text features, understanding of key ideas, or the ability to answer text-dependent questions. For the purposes of this illustration, we selected Reading Anchor Standard 5 for Information Text: Know and use various text features (e.g., headings, tables of contents, glossaries, electronic menus, icons) to locate key facts or information in a text. To design a formative assessment of students' text comprehension, we focus assessment tasks on one of the macro text elements noted above—text structure or text features, key ideas, or answering text-dependent questions—or a combination of them.

For the purposes of this example, we ask students to use a glossary to find a series of **bolded** words in the text in order to locate key facts or information. While this assessment appears to target the microstructure feature of word comprehension, it actually is assessing student ability to recognize and use a macro text feature, in this case the glossary. To assess comprehension of macrostructure, a teacher would want to test more than one feature. Teachers also need to construct a sufficient number of questions for each text feature, usually seven or more, so that failure to correctly answer one or two questions would not lead to an erroneous conclusion that students aren't comprehending text at the macro-processing or global text organizational level.

Figure 5.6. Macro-Level Comprehension Formative Assessment Tasks

Example Set 1: The Chocolate Is Poured

The chocolate is poured into **molds**. Molds are used to shape things. The chocolate is cooled in the molds.

A **mold** is:

A. a bowl shaped like a disk.
B. a container used to shape chocolate.
C. a process that allows chocolate to cool.
D. a part of the chocolate-making process where the chocolate is still liquid.

Example Set 2: Cocoa Beans Grow

A farmer plants many cocoa trees. Hard **pods** grow on each tree. Inside each pod are seeds called cocoa beans.

A **pod** is:

A. a group of student desks put together in a classroom.
B. a protective covering like a bandage.
C. hard growths or lumps on the limbs of a cocoa tree.
D. fruits of a cocoa tree.

Several examples of glossary use for word knowledge assessment tasks developed from the title *From Cocoa Beans to Chocolate* (Nelson, 2003) are displayed in Figure 5.6.

After allowing students time to read the entire text *From Cocoa Bean to Chocolate* (Nelson, 2003), the teacher asks students to mark the correct answer for the bolded word. They are instructed, after having selected their responses, to consult the glossary provided in the text to confirm or correct their answers. For students to score satisfactorily on this task, they should receive a score of 100%. Teachers should note the types of errors students make to determine what types of problems, if any, students may be having at the macro–text–processing level.

There are many types of formative assessment tasks that could be constructed for the macro level of the CI Model's construction processing. Figure 5.2 illustrates several formative comprehension assessment tasks at the macro-processing level for story or text features, structures, key ideas, and answering text-dependent questions.

Using our same informational book title, *From Cocoa Beans to Chocolate* (Nelson, 2003), we provide additional examples of formative assessment tasks that could be used to assess students' macro-level text construction processing linked to the CCSS Reading Anchor Standards.

Having already illustrated assessment tasks for Standard 7, we provide illustrations of alternative formative comprehension assessment tasks for other CCSS Reading Standards that pertain to the macro-level processes (key ideas and global coherence), as described in the CI Model.

The first alternative formative assessment approach is the use of "cloze" graphic organizers. Reutzel (1986a, 1986b) first described the use of cloze story mapping, where a partially completed graphic organizer that represents story structure is filled in by students after reading a story text. In the case of our informational text example, every third concept/key idea circle is left empty for the student to fill in as an assessment of macro text processing (see Figure 5.7). To meet CCSS Reading Anchor Standard 5, students use the text feature of bolded headings, to fill in the missing information in the text structure graphic.

The second alternative assessment is a text feature and text structure identification task. In this task, students first are asked to carefully look through a book to identify whether it is literature (story or poem) or informational text. Next, students are to look for listed text features using the attached checklist under the properly identified text type, story, or informational text. In the case of the title *From Cocoa Bean to Chocolate* (Nelson, 2003), the use of this checklist should result in the students' correctly linking the features of this informational text to the author's text structure—sequential/procedural (see Figure 5.8).

Another example of assessing students' comprehension at the macro–text–processing level is to use text-dependent questions to assess understanding of key ideas in text. Text-dependent questions intended to probe macro text understandings require students to read across sentences to locate answers. We provide two examples of text-dependent questions using the text *From Cocoa Bean to Chocolate* (Nelson, 2003).

Text-Dependent Question 1:

What processes make taking the shells off cocoa beans easier?

Text-Dependent Question 2:

What process makes chocolate creamy and smooth?

Step 4: Constructing Integration-Level Comprehension Assessment Tasks for CCSS Reading Anchor Standards

To prepare integration-level comprehension assessment tasks to address the CCSS for reading informational text, we once again consult Figure

Figure 5.7. Cloze Graphic Organizer

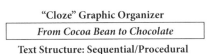

"Cloze" Graphic Organizer

From Cocoa Bean to Chocolate

Text Structure: Sequential/Procedural

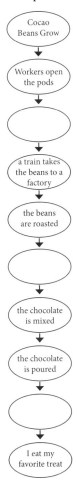

5.2. We note several assessment tasks we could ask students to perform to indicate that they can integrate the information constructed from the text, coupled with their background knowledge, to provide a reasonable and reasoned interpretation of the text. For purposes of this example, we selected Reading Anchor Standard 7 for Informational Text: Explain how specific images contribute to and clarify a text.

Figure 5.8. Text Feature Checklist to Identify Text or Story Structure

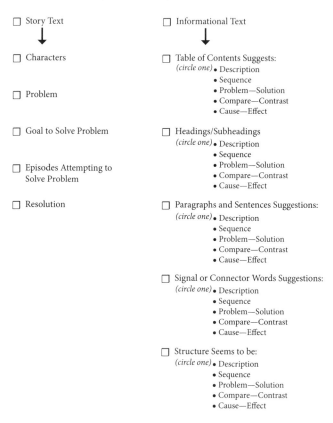

To design this level of formative assessment tasks, we focus on those integration tasks listed at level 3 of the CI Model in Figure 5.2. In this specific example, we ask students to describe the process of a cocoa bean becoming chocolate by requiring them to sequence a series of images taken from a Google image search on the Internet. When designing an assessment task such as this, teachers select a sufficient number of illustrations, usually seven or more, so that a student's failure to correctly sequence one or two illustrations would not lead to the erroneous conclusion that the student isn't able to describe how illustrations can be properly sequenced in order to demonstrate the ability to integrate text-based information with background knowledge to create a situation model of the text. Sequencing illustrations to describe the sequential process of a how a cocoa bean is made into chocolate is an excellent example of an integration-level comprehension assessment task. Students are told that they are to use what they have learned from reading *From Cocoa Bean to Chocolate* (Nelson, 2003) to arrange each picture into the sequence representing how cocoa beans become chocolate. For students to score satisfactorily on this task, they should receive a score of 100%, especially if look backs at the text are permitted to check the sequence. Teachers note the types of errors students make on this picture-sequencing assessment task to determine what types of problems, if any, students may be having at the integration text-processing level. Younger students should be encouraged to use the text to confirm their sequential arrangement of the pictures to represent the process for making cocoa beans into chocolate.

At the conclusion of the integration phase of the CI Model–based assessment process, students could be asked to correct any sequential errors and then use the sequenced series of pictures or images, along with providing descriptive labels for each illustration, to create a diagram of the chocolate-making process. After doing so, students could make an oral presentation to a small group, a peer, a parent, or an older student, using their diagram of the process to teach about how chocolate gets made from cocoa beans. This final product, the diagram, and the process of teaching another person, could be evaluated by the small-group members, a peer, a parent, or an older child using a simple rubric, as shown in Figure 5.9.

Another alternative assessment task at the integration level of comprehension processing is to have students write a summary. Still another alternative assessment task could be to ask students to write several text-dependent questions to use in an interview with other students in order to elicit the process by which a cocoa bean becomes chocolate.

ASSESSING MASTERY OF THE ANCHOR STANDARDS: A CLASSROOM ILLUSTRATION

In this classroom example, we describe the process one teacher used to create formative assessment tasks using the CI Model of Text Comprehension as a guide for the systematic selection and assessment of the CCSS Reading Anchor Standards for Literature and Informational Text. A 2nd-grade teacher, Mr. Waxler, has been planning to conduct

Figure 5.9. Rubric for Scoring a Diagram

1. *Title* clearly labels the focus or purpose
        Yes   No
        1 pt.   0 pt.

2. *Parts* of the diagram are clearly illustrated and labeled
        Yes   No
        1 pt.   0 pt.

3. *Diagram* is designed to communicate relationship of ideas to one another, for example, cycle, description, sequence, compare-contrast, and so on.
        Yes   No
        1 pt.   0 pt.

4. *Diagram* is legible, organized, and clearly presented.
        Yes   No
        1 pt.   0 pt.

5. *Information* in diagram is accurate and current (up-to-date).
        Yes   No
        1 pt.   0 pt.

TOTAL: _____
A score of five is the anticipated outcome for this assessment.

a benchmark assessment of his students' mastery of the CCSS Anchor Standards for reading informational text. Mr. Waxler begins his formative comprehension assessment task planning by consulting cluster 4 and Anchor Standard 10 of the CCSS Reading Anchor Standards: By the end of the year, read and comprehend [literature/informational texts] with prompting and support (K–1) *or* at the high end of the grade level text complexity band independently and proficiently (2–3). The most recently assessed text genre in his 1st-grade classroom was selected from the literature genre. Consequently, he selects the next text from the informational text genre in order to balance text genres between literature and informational text. Next, he decides that he can maximize motivation by looking for an informational text that relates to a topic or theme similar to the topic or theme of the literature book students previously read, *Frog and Toad Are Friends* (Lobel, 1971a). After searching in his school's library, he locates an informational text by J. Kottke titled *From Tadpole to Frog* (2000).

To determine whether the text he tentatively selected is appropriately challenging for a grade-level assessment at the end of the 1st-grade year, he searched the Lexile.com website for the title *From Tadpole to Frog* (Kottke, 2000). The Lexile level of this title was 380L, situated below 420L, the lowest end of the grade 2 Lexile level.

Next, he read the text closely to identify potential qualitative comprehension supports or obstacles to be faced by his 1st-grade students when they read this text as an assessment. The supports/obstacles he noted in this book included: use of a glossary to locate meanings for bolded words; full-color photographs without captions; an index; infrequent use of signal words to cue connections among ideas or text structure; but no bolded headings or subheadings, and no diagrams or illustrations that show the entire life cycle from tadpole to frog.

Assessing Microstructure to Construct a Textbase

After selecting *From Tadpole to Frog* (Kottke, 2000) as an appropriately challenging text for end-of-year assessment, he carefully reread this informational text to plan his selection of multiple CCSS Reading Anchor Standards to assess the multiple levels of text comprehension processing described in the CI Model. Mr. Waxler determined that Reading Anchor Standard 3: Describe the connection between two individuals, events, ideas or pieces of information in a text, would be the starting point for designing his formative comprehension assessment task at the microstructure level of text processing. Using *From Tadpole to Frog* (Kottke, 2000), he developed several assessment items in which students must demonstrate the ability to meet the expectations of Reading Anchor Standard 3 by answering several maze questions probing the use of cohesion terms to connect ideas in text. Examples of Mr. Waxler's formative micro-level comprehension tasks assessing cohesion connections at the micro level of textbase construction are found in Figure 5.10.

In this assessment task, Mr. Waxler assessed his students' abilities to connect ideas in sentences to one another using cohesion terms or signal words. Students should be able to perform this task with 100% accuracy. With time and practice, Mr. Waxler can increase the difficulty of this assessment task by using a maze assessment task in which students fill in the missing cohesion connection term rather than selecting the correct one from a stack of options.

A frog egg is laid in a pond. _____, the egg becomes a tadpole.

Figure 5.10. Micro-Processing Level of CI Model of Text Comprehension: Example of Maze Assessment for Reading Anchor Standard 3

Next,

1. A frog egg is laid in a pond. **First,** the egg becomes a tadpole.

Last,

Before
2. **After** a tadpole hatches from an egg, it begins to grow legs.
Then
Because
3. Its tail becomes shorter. Its eyes and mouth grow larger. **Then** the tadpole looks more and more like a frog.

Before

is an example of a maze cohesion connection term. An appropriate set of connector terms must be supplied in the blank by the student such as, *then*, *second*, *next*, *after that*, and so on.

Assessing Macrostructure to Construct a Textbase

At the macro level of textbase construction in the CI Model, Mr. Waxler determined that his students should demonstrate their ability to meet the expectations of Reading Anchor Standard 5: Know and use various text features (e.g., headings, tables of contents, glossaries, electronic menus, icons) to locate key facts or information in text. To assess his students' ability to meet this standard using *From Tadpole to Frog* (Kottke, 2000), Mr. Waxler asked his students to locate specific information using a common text feature—an index. An example of a macro–level–comprehension–processing assessment task linked to Reading Anchor Standard 5 is shown in Figure 5.11.

In this assessment, students must use the index to answer text-dependent questions about key facts in an informational text and document the page number(s) in the text where the answer is found.

Assessing the Integration of a Situation Model

Advancing from the construction phase to the integration phase of the CI Model, Mr. Waxler considered how he might assess his students' abilities to create a situation model or interpretation of the text *From Tadpole to Frog* (Kottke, 2000). He consulted Figure 5.2 once again to determine which of the specific CCSS Reading Anchor Standards listed address this level of text comprehension processing. As a culminating assessment task,

Figure 5.11. Macro-Processing Level of CI Model of Text Comprehension: Example of Text Feature Use Assessment Task for Reading Anchor Standard 5

Find the index on page 24 of *From Tadpole to Frog* (Kottke, 2000). Look up the **bolded** word(s) in the index to find the information needed to answer the following questions:

A frog **egg** laid in a pond looks like:

A. a rock
B. a stick
C. a brown bug
D. a black dot
Page number where the answer is found _____.

A **tadpole** _____ from its egg.

A. is born
B. hatches
C. jumps
D. crawls
Page number where the answer is found ____.

---

he selected Reading Anchor Standard 9: Identify basic similarities in and differences between two texts on the same topic.

For this assessment task, Mr. Waxler located another similarly challenging text on the topic of frogs that his students previously had read with him during a shared reading. The title of this text was *Frogs!* (Carney, 2009), a *Kids National Geographic* informational text. The Lexile level of this book is 410L, at the upper end of the end-of-year Lexile level stretch bandwidth but below 420L, the lower end of the grade 2 Lexile level.

In this final assessment task, students are given both texts, *From Tadpole to Frog* (Kottke, 2000) and *Frogs!* (Carney, 2009), to read aloud. They are instructed to read the texts aloud and then to fill in missing information from the two texts in a graphic organizer, as shown in Figure 5.12.

To wrap up this formative comprehension assessment cycle, Mr. Waxler carefully notes strengths and weakness in his students' performance of each of the formative comprehension assessment tasks. He notes his students' performance at various levels of the text comprehension process, as described in the CI Model. He also makes note of which specific CCSS reading standards his students have mastered and those for which they may need additional instructional support, guidance, and practice. He keeps data in a computer spreadsheet. He color-codes each

Figure 5.12. Graphic Organizer for Compare/Contrast

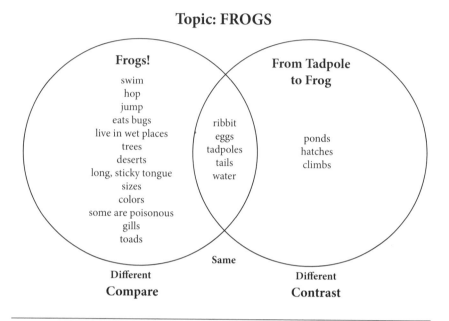

text–comprehension–processing level and each specific CCSS Reading Anchor Standard for mastery (green) and/or additional instructional attention (yellow). (See example spreadsheet available at www.tcpress.com.) The formative assessment tasks that Mr. Waxler has designed can be given to a whole class if sufficient copies of the assessment texts are available. He also can administer his assessment tasks in small groups where he can observe his students carefully as they complete each formative assessment task.

ADAPTING COMPREHENSION INSTRUCTION USING DATA FROM FORMATIVE ASSESSMENTS

The purpose of designing comprehension formative assessment tasks is to provide teachers, administrators, and coaches data to inform the design of subsequent comprehension instruction (Afflerbach, 2012). To illustrate how formative assessments can be used to inform subsequent design of comprehension instruction, we turn to the case data of a 2nd-grade child named Zarita (pseudonym) who has completed a series of formative assessment tasks in comprehension. We display in Figure 5.13 a summary

Figure 5.13. A Summary Performance Report of Zarita's Completion of Three Formative Comprehension Assessment Tasks

Task 1: Construction—Micro Processing

- Word-Level Maze Task
- CCSS I1: Answer questions about key details

86% correct—missed item #2 on the meaning of *mold*

Task 2: Construction—Macro Processing

- Text Structure Cloze Graphic Organizer Task
- CCSS I5: Use text features to locate key facts

90% correct—missed item #9—heading *the chocolate is wrapped*

Task 3: Integration—Situation Model

- Create a Diagram of Process
- CCSS I7: Use Illustrations and Key Ideas to Describe a Text

100% correct—pictures with labels properly sequenced in diagram

---

report of Zarita's performance on three formative comprehension assessment tasks after reading the already familiar text *From Cocoa Bean to Chocolate* (Nelson, 2003).

A careful examination of Zarita's summary performance report reveals some areas where additional support during subsequent small-group instruction may be helpful. At the micro-processing level, Zarita may benefit from a teacher-guided demonstration of how to think about what would make sense in a maze assessment task at the word-meaning level. The teacher might also help Zarita to note that when a word isn't known, particularly a bolded word in an informational text, the word meaning can be looked up in the glossary to help with selecting or confirming the correct response to a maze task.

Zarita also might be scaffolded to attend carefully to bolded headings and match these to entries in tables of contents. When asked to provide a sequential listing of the contents of text, as was required in the cloze graphic organizer task, a teacher could model how all of the other entries displayed in the cloze graphic organizer were taken in order from the table of contents and/or the bolded headings in the book. Demonstrating this match helps students to make better use of text features to improve their comprehension of text.

Finally, Zarita was able to produce, after sequencing illustrations and labeling them, an articulate presentation of how key ideas and illustrations could be used to describe the contents and sequence of a text. Zarita was careful to check her picture sequence and the necessary labels with each illustration and heading in the book. From this Zarita has learned where authors place top-level ideas in information text and how pictures are used to complement the written information so as to clarify text descriptions and concepts.

When teachers carefully examine the results of these formative comprehension assessment tasks, they are able to determine whether there are consistent patterns within a student's performance over time indicating a struggle with one or more levels of the comprehension process. In addition, teachers can determine which of the Reading Anchor Standards over time may still pose a challenge to a student. As teachers collect these data, they can note levels of comprehension processing and/or performance on specific CCSS Reading Anchor Standards with which individual and small groups of students continue to struggle. After noting these patterns, teachers can use this information to inform subsequent lesson design for the whole class or for small groups of students who struggle with similar levels of comprehension processing and/or performing particular tasks under the CCSS Reading Anchor Standards.

In summary, we have described in this final chapter how teachers can design and use formative comprehension assessment tasks to assess their students' levels of text comprehension processing, as described in the CI Model, and their mastery of specific CCSS Anchor Standards for reading literature and informational text. We also described how teachers can use formative assessment data to adapt and modify comprehension lessons in order to provide extended support for students who struggle.

Using the CI Model as a lens or framework, as described throughout this book, provides teachers, coaches, administrators, and researchers with a theoretically grounded system for designing comprehension instruction and assessment in the age of the Common Core State Standards (NGA Center & CCSSO, 2010). Finally, using data gathered from administrations of these formative comprehension assessment tasks, teachers, administrators, coaches, and other interested education professionals can gain insights into how to provide subsequent, targeted comprehension instruction to support students' continued growth and progress toward becoming competent and confident readers who routinely engage in the virtuous cycle of reading comprehension—using world knowledge to comprehend text, and using text to build new knowledge.

Children's Literature Cited

Anthony, J. (2014). *The dandelion seed's big dream*. Nevada City, NY: Dawn Publications.

Berger, M. & Berger, G. (2004). *Autumn*. New York, NY: Scholastic, Inc.

Carney, E. (2009). *Frogs!* Washington, DC: National Geographic Kids.

Christelow, E. (2004). *Five little monkeys bake a birthday cake*. New York, NY: Clarion Books.

Cleary, B. (1965). *The mouse and the motorcycle*. New York, NY: HarperCollins.

Clyne, M., & Griffiths, R. (2005). *Sand*. Parsippany, NJ: Celebration Press–Pearson Education Group.

Daronco, M. & Presti, L. (2011). *Measuring tools*. New Rochelle, NY: Benchmark Education Company.

Freeman, M. (2007). *Watching the weather*. Marlborough, MA: Sundance Newbridge Educational Publishing.

Ginsburg, M. (1974). *Mushroom in the rain*. New York, NY, Macmillan. Audio book available at www.audiobooks.com/audiobook/mushroom-in-the-rain/138392

Kottke, J. (2000). *From tadpole to frog*. New York, NY: Children's Press.

Lobel, A. (1971a). *Frog and toad are friends*. New York, NY: HarperCollins.

Lobel, A. (1971b). *Frog and toad together*. New York, NY: HarperCollins.

Matsumoto, L. (1996). *Beyond 'Ohi'a Valley: Adventures in a Hawaiian rainforest*. Honolulu, HI: Lehua, Inc.

Minarik, E. H. (1957). *Little bear*. New York, NY: HarperCollins.

Nelson, R. (2003). *From cocoa bean to chocolate*. Minneapolis, MN: Lerner.

Parkes, B. (1998). *Using tools*. Marlborough, MA: Sundance Newbridge Educational Publishing.

Parrish, P. (1991). *Amelia Bedelia*. New York, NY: HarperCollins.

Rawls, W. W. (1961). *Where the red fern grows*. New York, NY: Doubleday Books for Young Readers.

Rey, H. A. (1998). *Curious George goes to a chocolate factory*. Boston, MA: Houghton Mifflin.

Rylant, C. (1987). *Henry and Mudge: The first book of their adventures*. New York, NY: Simon & Schuster.

Sendak, M. (1963). *Where the wild things are*. New York, NY: Harper and Row.

Underwood, D. (2010). *Hiding in rain forests* (Creature Camouflage). North Mankato, MN: Heinemann-Raintree.

Weiss, E. (2008). *From seed to dandelion*. New York, NY: Children's Press.

White, E. B. (1952). *Charlotte's web*. New York, NY: HarperCollins.

References

Afflerbach, P. (2012). *Understanding and using reading assessment, K–12* (2nd ed.). Newark, DE: International Reading Association.

Allington, R. L. (2009). If they don't read much … 30 years later. In E. H. Hiebert (Ed.), *Reading more, reading better* (pp. 30–54). New York, NY: Guilford Publishers.

Anderson, R. C., & Pearson, P. D. (1981). A schema-theoretic view of basic processes in reading. In P. D. Pearson, R. Barr, M. L. Kamil, & P. Mosenthal (Eds.), *Handbook of reading research* (Vol. 1, pp. 255–292). New York, NY: Longman.

Baddeley, A. D., & Hitch, G. J. (2000). Development of working memory: Should the Pascual-Leone and the Baddeley and Hitch models be merged? *Journal of Experimental Child Psychology, 77*(2), 128–137.

Barone, D. (2015). Challenging background knowledge within children's literature. *Childhood Education, 91*, 16–23.

Beers, K., & Probst, R. E. (2012). *Notice and note: Strategies for close reading.* Portsmouth, NH: Heinemann.

Berkowitz, S., & Taylor, B. (1981). The effects of text type and familiarity on the nature of information recalled by readers. In M. L. Kamil (Ed.), *Directions in reading: Research and instruction* (pp. 157–161). Washington, DC: National Reading Conference.

Block, C., & Mangieri, J. (2002). Recreational reading: 20 years later. *The Reading Teacher, 55*, 572–580.

Cain, K., Oakhill, J., & Lemmon, K. (2004). Individual differences in the inference of word meanings from context: The influence of reading comprehension, vocabulary knowledge, and memory capacity. *Journal of Educational Psychology, 96*(4), 671–681. doi: 10.1037/0022-0663.96.4.671

Casteel, M. A., & Simpson, G. B. (1991). Textual coherence and the development of inferential generation skills. *Journal of Research in Reading, 14*(2), 116–129 .

Catts, H. W., Fey, M. E., Tomblin J. B., & Zhang, X. (2002). A longitudinal investigation of reading outcomes in children with language impairments. *Journal of Speech, Language, and Hearing Research, 45*, 1142–1157. doi: 10.1044/1092-4388(2002/093)

Catts, H. W., Fey, M. E., Zhang, X., & Tomblin, J. B. (1999). Language basis of reading and reading disabilities: Evidence from a longitudinal investigation. *Scientific Studies of Reading*, 3, 331–361. doi: 10.1207/s1532799xssr0304_2

Chall, J. S., Jacobs, V. A., & Baldwin, L. E. (1990). *The reading crisis: Why poor children fall behind.* Cambridge, MA: Harvard University Press.

Children's books in print, 2015. (2016). Armenia, NY: Grey House.

Clarke, P., Snowling, M., Truelove, E., & Hulme, C. (2010). Ameliorating children's reading-comprehension difficulties: A randomized controlled trial. *Psychological Science, 2*(8), 1106–1116. doi: 10.1177/0956797610375449

Cummins, S. (2013). *Close reading of informational texts: Assessment-driven instruction in grades 3–8.* New York, NY: Guilford Press.

Cunningham, P. M., & Allington, R. L. (1999). *Classrooms that work: They can all read and write.* Reading, MA: Addison Wesley Longman, Inc.

Davis, F. (1944). Fundamental factors of comprehension in reading. *Psychometrika, 9*(3), 185–197.

Dennis, D. V. (2009). "I'm not stupid": How assessment drives (in)appropriate reading instruction. *Journal of Adolescent and Adult Literacy Instruction, 53*(4), 283–290.

Dickinson, D. K., & Tabors, P. O. (Eds.). (2001). *Beginning literacy with language: Young children learning at home and school.* Baltimore, MD: Brookes.

Dougherty-Stahl, K. A. (2009). Assessing the comprehension of young children. In S. E. Israel & G. G. Duffy (Eds.), *Handbook of research on reading comprehension* (pp. 428–448). New York, NY: Routledge.

Duff, F., & Clarke, P. (2011). Practitioner review: Reading disorders: What are the effective interventions and how should they be implemented and evaluated? *Journal of Child Psychology and Psychiatry, 52*(1), 3–12. doi:10.1111/j.1469-7610.2010.02310.x

Duke, N. K. (2000). 3.6 minutes per day: The scarcity of informational texts in first grade. *Reading Research Quarterly, 35*, 202–224.

Duke, N. K. (2002). *Improving comprehension of informational text.* Presentation at the Center for Improvement of Early Reading Achievement Summer Institute, Ann Arbor, MI.

Duke, N. K. (2005). Comprehension of what for what: Comprehension as a nonunitary construct. In S. G. Paris & S. A. Stahl (Eds.), *Children's reading comprehension and assessment* (pp. 93–106). Mahwah, NJ: Erlbaum.

Duke, N. K., Cartwright, K. B., & Hilden, K. R. (2014). Difficulties with reading comprehension. In C. A. Stone, E. R. Silliman, B. J. Ehren, & G. P. Wallach (Eds.), *Handbook of language and literacy: Development and disorders* (2nd ed., pp. 451–468). New York, NY: Guilford Press.

Duke, N. K., Halliday, J. L., & Roberts, K. L. (2013). Reading standards for informational text. In L. M. Morrow, T. Shanahan, & K. K. Wixson (Eds.), *Teaching with the common core standards for English language arts, PreK–2* (pp. 46–66). New York, NY: Guilford Press.

Duke, N. K., Pearson, P. D., Strachan, S. L., & Billman, A. K. (2011). Essential elements of fostering and teaching reading comprehension. In S. J. Samuels & A. E. Farstrup (Eds.), *What research has to say about reading instruction* (4th ed., pp. 51–93). Newark, DE: International Reading Association.

Durkin, D. (1993). *Teaching them to read* (6th ed.). Boston, MA: Allyn & Bacon.

Eisenberg, S. L., Ukrainetz, T. A., Hsu, J. R., Kaderavek, J. N., Justice, L. A., & Gillam, R. B. (2008). Noun phrase elaboration in children's spoken stories. *Language Speech and Hearing Services in Schools, 39*(2), 145–157. doi: 10.1044/0161-1461(2008/014)

Finneran, D., & Leonard, L. (2011). Role of linguistic input in third person singular –s use in the speech of young children. *Journal of Speech, Language, and Hearing Research, 53*, 1065–1074.

Fisher, D., & Frey, N. (2012). Close reading in elementary schools. *The Reading Teacher, 66*(3), 179–188. doi: 10.1002/TRTR.01117

Frey, N., & Fisher, D. (2013). *Rigorous reading: 5 access points for comprehending complex texts.* Thousand Oaks, CA: Corwin Press.

Gajria, M., & Salvia, J. (1992). The effects of summarization instruction on text comprehension of students with learning disabilities. *Exceptional Children, 58,* 508–516.

Gillam, S., Hartzheim, D., Studenka, B., Simonsmeier, V., & Gillam, R. (2015). Narrative intervention for children with Autism Spectrum Disorder (ASD). *Journal of Speech, Language and Hearing Research,* 1–14.

Gillam, R., Montgomery, J., & Gillam, S. (2009). Memory and attention in children with language impairments. In R. G. Schwartz (Ed.), *Handbook of child language disorders* (pp. 201–125). New York, NY: Psychology Press.

Gillam, S., & Gillam, R. (2014). Improving clinical services: Be aware of fuzzy connections between principles and strategies. *Language, Speech, and Hearing Services in Schools, 45,* 137–144.

Gillam, S., Gillam, R., & Reece, K. (2012). Language outcomes of contextualized and decontextualized language intervention: Results of an early efficacy study. *Language, Speech, and Hearing Services in Schools, 43,* 1–44. doi:10.1044/0161-1461(2011/11-0022)

Gillam, S., & Reutzel, D. R. (2013). Common core state standards (CCSS): New directions for enhancing young children's oral language development. In L. M. Morrow, T. Shanahan, & K. K. Wixson (Eds.), *Teaching with the Common Core Standards for English Language Arts, PreK–2* (pp. 107–127). New York, NY: Guilford Press.

Graesser, A. C. (2007). An introduction to strategic reading comprehension. In D. S. McNamara (Ed.), *Reading comprehension strategies: Theories, interventions, and technologies* (pp. 3–26). New York, NY: Erlbaum.

Greenhalgh, K., & Strong, C. (2001). Literate language features in spoken narratives of children with typical language and children with language impairments. *Language, Speech, and Hearing Services in Schools, 32,* 114–125.

Hiebert, E. H. (2012, September). *It's not just informational text that supports knowledge acquisition: The critical role of narrative text in the common core state standards.* Retrieved from http://textproject.org/library/frankly-freddy/the-critical-role-of-narrative-text-in-the-common-core-state-standards

Hogan, T. P., Bridges, M. S., Justice, L. M., & Cain, K. (2011). Increasing higher level language skills to improve reading comprehension. *Focus on Exceptional Children, 44*(3), 1–20.

Jarmulowicz, L., & Hay, S. (2009). Derivational morphophonology: Exploring errors in third graders' productions. *Language, Speech, and Hearing Services in Schools, 40,* 299–311.

Jarmulowicz, L., Taran, V., & Hay, S. (2007). Third graders' metalinguistic skills, reading skills, and stress production in derived English words. *Journal of Speech, Language, and Hearing Research, 50,* 1593–1605.

Kamhi, A. G., & Catts, H. W. (2002). The language basis of reading: Implications for classification and treatment of children with reading disabilities. In K. G. Butler & E. R. Silliman (Eds.), *Speaking, reading, and writing in children with language learning disabilities in research and practice* (pp. 45–72). Mahwah, NJ: Erlbaum.

Kendeou, P., van den Broek, P., White, M., & Lynch, J. (2007). Comprehension in preschool and early elementary children: Skill development and strategy interventions. In D. S. McNamara (Ed.), *Reading comprehension strategies: Theories, interventions, and technologies* (pp. 27–46). New York, NY: Erlbaum.

Kintsch, W. (1998). *Comprehension: A paradigm for cognition.* New York, NY: Cambridge University Press.

Kintsch, W. (2004) The Construction–Integration model of text comprehension and its implications for instruction. In R. Ruddell & N. Unrau (Eds.), *Theoretical models and processes of reading* (5th ed.). Newark, DE: International Reading Association.

Kintsch, W. (2013). Revisiting the construction–integration model of text comprehension and its implications for instruction. In D. E. Alvermann, N. J. Unrau, & R. B. Ruddell (Eds.), *Theoretical models and processes of reading* (6th ed., pp. 807–839). Newark, DE: International Reading Association.

Kintsch, W., & Kintsch, E. (2005). Comprehension. In S. G. Paris & S. A. Stahl (Eds.), *Children's reading comprehension and assessment* (pp. 71–104). Mahwah, NJ: Erlbaum.

Kintsch, W., & van Dijk, T. A. (1978). Toward a model of discourse comprehension and production. *Psychological Review, 85,* 363–394.

Kucan, L., Hapgood, S., & Palincsar, A. S. (2011). Teachers' specialized knowledge for supporting student comprehension in text-based discussions. *The Elementary School Journal, 112*(1), 61–82.

Langer, J. A. (2011). *Envisioning literature: Literary understanding and literature instruction* (2nd ed.). New York, NY: Teachers College Press.

Langer, J. A., Applebee, A. N., Mullis, I. V. S., & Foertsch, M. A. (1990). *Learning to read in our nation's schools: Instruction and achievement in 1988 at grades 4, 8, and 12.* Princeton, NJ: Educational Testing Service.

Leonard, L. (1998). *Children with specific language impairment.* Cambridge, MA: MIT Press.

Lewin, K. (1951). *Field theory in social science: Selected theoretical papers* (D. Cartwright, Ed.). New York, NY: Harper & Row.

Lewis, W. E., Walpole, S., & McKenna, M. C. (2014). *Cracking the common core: Choosing and using texts in grades 6–12.* New York, NY: Guilford Press.

Maratsos, M. (1990). Are actions to verbs as objects are to nouns? On the differential semantic bases of form, class, category. *Linguistics, 28,* 1351–1379.

McKenna, M. C., & Stahl, K.A.D. (2009). *Assessment for reading instruction* (2nd ed.). New York, NY: Guilford Press.

McLaughlin, M., & Overturf, B. J. (2013*). The common core: Teaching K–5 students to meet the reading standards.* Newark, DE: International Reading Association.

McNamara, D. S. (2009). The importance of teaching reading strategies. *Perspectives on Language and Literacy, 35,* 34–38, 40.

Meyer, B.J.F. (1975). *The organization of prose and its effects on memory.* Amsterdam, Netherlands: North Holland.

Meyer, B. & Wijukumar, K. (2007). A web-based tutoring system for the structure strategy: theoretical background, design, and findings. In D. S. McNamara (Ed.), *Reading comprehension strategies: Theories, interventions, and technologies* (pp. 347–374). New York, NY: Lawrence Erlbaum.

Mintz, T. H., Newport, E. L., & Bever, T. G. (2002). The distributional structure of grammatical categories in speech to young children. *Cognitive Science, 26,* 393–424.

Morrow, L. M., Tracey, D. H., & Healey, K. M. (2013). Reading standards for literature: Developing comprehension. In L. M. Morrow, T. Shanahan, & K. K. Wixson (Eds.), *Teaching with the common core standards for English language arts, PreK–2* (pp. 22–45). New York, NY: Guilford Press.

Nation, K., Cocksey, J., Taylor, J.S.H., & Bishop, D.V.M. (2010). A longitudinal investigation of early reading and language skills in children with poor reading comprehension. *Journal of Child Psychology and Psychiatry, 51*, 1031–1039.

National Assessment of Educational Progress. (2011). *Reading framework for the 2011 National Assessment of Educational Progress.* Washington, DC: U.S. Department of Education.

National Early Literacy Panel. (2008). *Developing early literacy: Report of the National Early Literacy Panel.* Washington, DC: National Institute for Literacy. Retrieved from https://www.nichd.nih.gov/publications/pubs/documents/NELPReport09.pdf#search=National%20Early%20Literacy%20Panel

National Governors Association Center for Best Practices & Council of Chief State School Officers. (2010). *Common core state standards.* Retrieved from www.corestandards.org/

National Institute for Literacy. (2007). *What content-area teachers should know about adolescent literacy* (An interagency report by the National Institute for Literacy, National Institute for Child Health and Human Development, & U.S. Department of Education's Office for Vocational and Adult Education). Washington, DC: Government Printing Office.

National Institute of Child Health and Human Development. (2000). *Teaching children to read: An evidence-based assessment of the scientific research literature on reading and its implications for reading instruction* (NIH Publication No. 0-4754). Retrieved from https://www.nichd.nih.gov/publications/pubs/nrp/Pages/report.aspx

Neuman, S. B., & Roskos, K. (2012). Helping children become more knowledgeable through text. *The Reading Teacher, 66*, 207–210.

Oakhill, J., & Cain, K. (2012). The precursors of reading ability in young readers: Evidence from a four-year longitudinal study. *Scientific Studies of Reading, 16*, 91–121.

Olson, M. W. (1985). Text type and reader ability: The effects of paraphrase and text-based inference questions. *Journal of Reading Behavior, 17*, 199–214.

Paquette, K., Fello, S., & Jalongo, M. (2007). The talking drawings strategy: Using primary children's illustrations and oral language to improve comprehension of expository text. *Early Childhood Education Journal, 35*(1), 65–73. doi: 10.1007/s10643-007-0184-5

Paris, A. H., & Paris, S. G. (2003). Assessing narrative comprehension in young children. *Reading Research Quarterly, 38*, 36–76.

Pearson, P. D. (1974). Effects of grammatical complexity on children's comprehension, recall, and conception of certain semantic relations. *Reading Research Quarterly, 10*(2), 155–192.

Pearson, P. D., & Duke, N. (2002). Comprehension instruction in the primary grades. In C. C. Block & M. Pressley (Eds.), *Comprehension instruction: Research-based best practices* (pp. 247–258). New York, NY: Guilford Press.

Pearson, P. D., & Fielding, L. (1991). Comprehension instruction. In R. Barr, M. L. Kamil, P. Mosenthal, & P. D. Pearson (Eds.), *Handbook of reading research* (Vol. 2, pp. 815–860). New York, NY: Longman.

Pearson, P. D., & Hiebert, E. H. (2015). *Research-based practice for teaching common core literacy.* New York, NY: Teachers College Press.

Perfetti, C., & Stafura, J. (2014). Word knowledge in a theory of reading comprehension. *Scientific Studies of Reading, 18*(1), 22–37.

Potocki, A., Ecalle, J., & Magnan, A. (2013). Narrative comprehension skills in 5-year-old children: Correlational analysis and comprehender profiles. *The Journal of Educational Research, 106,* 14–26.

Pressley, M. (2001). What should comprehension instruction be the instruction of? In M. L. Kamil, P. B. Mosenthal, P. D. Pearson, & R. Barr (Eds.), *Handbook of reading research* (Vol. III, pp. 545–562). Mahwah, NJ: Erlbaum.

Raphael, T. (2000). Balancing literature and instruction: Lessons from the Book Club Project. In B. Taylor, M. Graves, & P. van den Broek (Eds.), *Reading for meaning: Fostering comprehension in the middle grades* (pp. 70–94). New York, NY: Teachers College Press.

Redington, M., Chater, N., & Finch, S. (1998). Distributional information: A powerful cue for acquiring syntactic categories. *Cognitive Science, 22,* 425–469.

Reutzel, D. R. (1986a, February). Clozing in on comprehension: The cloze story map. *The Reading Teacher, 39,* 524–528.

Reutzel, D. R. (1986b, July/August). Investigating a synthesized comprehension instructional strategy: The cloze story map. *The Journal of Educational Research, 79,* 343–349.

Scott, C., & Nelson, N. (2009). Sentence combining assessment and intervention applications. *Perspectives on Language, Learning and Education, 16,* 14–20.

Scott, M. A. (Ed.). (1908). *The essays of Francis Bacon.* New York, NY: Charles Scribner's Sons.

Shanahan, T. (2014). Should we teach students at their reading levels? *Reading Today, 32*(2), 14–15.

Shanahan, T. (2015). What teachers should know about common core: A guide for the perplexed. *The Reading Teacher, 68*(8), 583–588.

Shanahan, T., Callison, K., Carriere, C., Duke, N. K., Pearson, P. D., Schatschneider, C., & Torgesen, J. (2010). *Improving reading comprehension in kindergarten through 3rd grade: A practice guide* (NCEE 2010-4038). Washington, DC: National Center for Education Evaluation and Regional Assistance, Institute of Education Sciences, U.S. Department of Education. Retrieved from ies.ed.gov/ncee/wwc/PracticeGuide.aspx?sid=14

Smith, N. B. (2002). *American reading instruction* (special edition). Newark, DE: International Reading Association.

Snow, C. E. (1993). Families as social contexts for literacy development. *New Directions for Child Development, 61,* 11–24.

Snow, C. E. (2002). *Reading for understanding: Toward an R&D program in reading comprehension.* Santa Monica, CA: RAND.

Snow, C. E., Burns, M. S., & Griffin, P. (Eds.). (1998). *Preventing reading difficulties in young children.* Washington, DC: National Academy Press.

Tabors, P. O., & Snow, C. E. (2001). Young bilingual children and early literacy development. In S. B. Neuman & D. K. Dickinson (Eds.), *Handbook of early literacy research* (pp. 159–178). New York, NY: Guilford Press.

Tomasello, M. (2003). Constructing a language: A usage-based theory of language acquisition. Cambridge, MA: Harvard University Press.

Tompkins, V., Guo, Y., & Justice, L. M. (2013). Inference generation, story comprehension and language in the preschool years. *Reading and Writing, 26,* 403–429.

Watanabe, L. M., & Hall-Kenyon, K. M. (2011). Improving young children's writing: The influence of story structure on kindergartners' writing complexity. *Literacy Research and Instruction, 50,* 272–293.

Watson, S., Gable, R., Gear, S., & Hughes, K. (2012). Evidence-based strategies for improving the reading comprehension of secondary students: Implications for students with learning disabilities. *Learning Disabilities Research & Practice, 27,* 79–89.

Westby, C., Culatta, B., Lawrence, B., & Hall-Kenyon, K. (2010). Summarizing expository texts. *Topics in Language Disorders, 30,* 275–287.

Whitehurst, G. J., & Lonigan, C. J. (2001). Emergent literacy: Development from pre-readers to readers. In S. B. Neuman & D. K. Dickinson (Eds.), *Handbook of early literacy* research (pp. 11–29). New York, NY: Guilford Press.

Wilkinson, I.A.G., & Son, E. H. (2011). A dialogic turn in research on learning and teaching to comprehend. In M. L. Kamil, P. D. Pearson, E. B, Moje, & P. P. Afflerbach (Eds.), *Handbook of reading research* (Vol. IV, pp. 359–387). New York, NY: Routledge.

Williams, J. P., Hall, K. M., & Lauer, K. D. (2004). Teaching expository text structure to young at-risk learners: Building the basics of comprehension instruction. *Exceptionality, 12*(3), 129–144.

Williams, J., Stafford, B., Lauer, K., Hall, K., & Pollini, S. (2009). Embedding reading comprehension training in content-area instruction. *Journal of Educational Psychology, 101,* 1–20.

Index

Text processing. *See* Comprehension
    processes
Text selection, 27, 29, 31–32, 52, 92, 96
    for assessment, 110–112, 114–115,
        126–127
    for informational texts, 85–87, 91, 96
    for literature, 63, 65–68, 72–73, 75–77
Text structures, 14, 57, 58, 60, 115, 122
    of informational texts, 84, 85–86, 87, 93
    recognizing, 58–59
Thorndike, E., 104
Tomasello, M., 46
Tomblin, J. B., 2, 37
Tompkins, V., 61
Tracey, D. H., 62
Truelove, E., 38

Underwood, D., 58

Van den Broek, P., 2
Van Dijk, T. A., 60, 84
Verb phrases, 44
Verbs, 46

Vertical structuring, 48–49
Vertical structuring assessment, 118
Virtuous cycle of comprehension, 19, 20,
    105
Vocabulary, specific, 39

Walpole, S., 107
Watanabe, L. M., 62
Watson, S., 38
Weiss, E., 96
Westby, C., 38
White, E. B., 62
White, M., 2
Whitehurst, G. J., 37
Wijkumar, K., 60
Wilkinson, I. A. G., 10
Williams, J., 60, 95, 99
Word knowledge assessment tasks, 120–121
Word order, 42
World knowledge. *See* Knowledge,
    background/world

Zhang, X., 2, 37

About the Authors

D. Ray Reutzel is Dean of the College of Education at the University of Wyoming. Previous to his current position, he was the Emma Eccles Jones Distinguished Professor and Endowed Chair of Early Literacy Education at Utah State University for 14 years. He is the author of more than 225 published research reports in top-tier research journals, articles, books, book chapters, and monographs. He is the co-author of the best-selling textbook on the teaching of reading, *Teaching Children to Read: The Teacher Makes the Difference* (7th ed., 2015). He has received more than $16.5 million in research/professional development funding. He has been active in securing legislative and private foundation gifts in excess of $25 million. He is a past editor of *Literacy Research and Instruction* and *The Reading Teacher* and the current executive editor of *The Journal of Educational Research*. He received the 1999 A. B. Herr Award and the 2013 ALER Laureate Award from the Association of Literacy Researchers and Educators. Dr. Reutzel served as president of the Association of Literacy Educators and Researchers (ALER) from 2006–2007. He was presented the John C. Manning Public School Service Award by the International Reading Association in May 2007 in Toronto, Canada, and served as a member of the Board of Directors of the International Reading Association from 2007–2010. Dr. Reutzel was a member of the Literacy Research Association's Board of Directors from 2012–2015 and is a member and recently elected President of the *International Reading Hall of Fame*.

Cindy D. Jones is an associate professor and Director of the Literacy Clinic in the Department of Teacher Education and Leadership at Utah State University, specializing in literacy education and classroom instruction. She works in public schools providing professional development in reading and writing instruction. Dr. Jones's research focuses on the relationship of reading, writing, and oral discourse and how this relationship can be applied to instruction to promote students' literacy development. She has published in major research and professional journals such as

The Reading Teacher, The Journal of Educational Research, Reading and Writing Quarterly, and *The Elementary School Journal.* Dr. Jones received the International Reading Association Outstanding Dissertation Finalist Award, the J. Estill Alexander Future Leaders in Literacy Award, the Jerry Johns Promising Researcher Award, and the EEJ College of Education and Human Services Researcher/Scholar of the Year Award.

Sarah K. Clark is an associate professor at Utah State University. She has been engaged in the education field for the past 25 years as a classroom teacher, author, researcher, and professor. Dr. Clark has published a research monograph, three book chapters, and over 35 books for classroom teachers' use. Dr. Clark has published more than 20 academic journal articles found in prestigious journals such as the *Journal of Teacher Education, The Reading Teacher, The Elementary School Journal,* and *The Journal of Educational Research.* Dr. Clark has been honored to receive multiple awards, including the Jerry Johns Promising Researcher of the Year Award from the Association of Literacy Educators and Researchers and the Teacher of the Year Award from the EEJ College of Education and Human Services at Utah State University. Dr. Clark enjoys spending her time in elementary classrooms providing support for both teachers and children alike.

Sandra Laing Gillam is a professor in the Department of Communicative Disorders and Deaf Education at Utah State University and current Vice President for Speech Language Pathology Practice for the American Speech Language and Hearing Association (ASHA). Since coming to Utah State, she has received numerous awards and honors, including being named ASHA Fellow, Outstanding Alumnus, Undergraduate Research Mentor of the Year, and Outstanding Researcher of the Year. She earned her BS and MS degrees in Speech Language Pathology and Audiology at Auburn University and began her career as a speech language pathologist in public schools. Dr. Gillam obtained her doctorate at the University of Memphis and began her academic career at the University of Alabama. She currently teaches courses in language development and disorders and professional issues. Her research interests include language and literacy impairments, diverse populations, and comprehension. Dr. Gillam has received funding for her research from the Institute of Education Sciences.